Bobby Flay Fit

Also by Bobby Flay

BOBBY FLAY

FIT

200 RECIPES FOR
A HEALTHY LIFESTYLE

Bobby Flay
with Stephanie Banyas
and Sally Jackson

CLARKSON POTTER/PUBLISHERS
NEW YORK

Library of Congress Cataloging-in-Publication Data
Names: Flay, Bobby, author. | Banyas, Stephanie, author. | Jackson, Sally, author.
Title: Bobby Flay fit: 200 recipes for a healthy lifestyle / Bobby Flay with Stephanie Banyas and Sally Jackson.
Description: New York : Clarkson Potter/Publishers, [2017]
Identifiers: LCCN 2016044398 (print) | LCCN 2016048550 (ebook) | ISBN 9780385345934 | ISBN 9780385345941 (ebook)
Subjects: LCSH: Cooking. | Health. | LCGFT: Cookbooks.
Classification: LCC TX642 .F53 2017 (print) | LCC TX642 (ebook) | DDC 641.5—dc23
LC record available at https://lccn.loc.gov/2016044398

ISBN 978-0-385-34593-4
eBook ISBN 978-0-385-34594-1

Printed in China

Book and cover design by Ian Dingman
Cover photograph by Ed Anderson

The font "Nitti Grotesk" is a trademark of Blue Monday, copyright © Blue Monday

10 9 8 7 6 5 4 3 2 1

First Edition

This book is dedicated to my daughter, Sophie, a vibrant young woman who has always embraced food to the core of her soul and has always thought of it as her friend.

You are a role model to other young women: you work hard, you play hard, and you celebrate your life around the table. Most notably, you're inclusive of everyone around you and that makes me especially proud to be your father.

xo

Dad

Contents

A Way of Life

I became a chef because I love food. I love all kinds of different cuisines, traveling to taste something I've never eaten before, discovering a new ingredient, making the same recipe over and over again until it's perfect—and then riffing on that to come up with something new. Food is the center of my universe.

In my twenties, I could skip breakfast, work all day at Mesa Grill, tasting everything here and there, drink lots of coffee, and then have a huge meal at the end of the day before passing out and doing it all over again. As I opened more restaurants and started filming television programs, I continued to eat whatever and whenever I wanted to fuel stress-filled, jam-packed days.

And then I turned forty. It wasn't an overnight change, but I definitely started to feel heavy and slow. My energy level plummeted. I didn't love what I saw in the mirror, either. I had to do something—something I could live with long term. I took a serious look at what I was eating, and when. I realized that I couldn't down two burgers and a shake for a late dinner the way I could in my twenties. But there's no way I was ever going to swear off any kind of food (and definitely not ice cream, my weakness).

I went back to basics, concentrating on fueling my body with nourishing, great-tasting food. I now eat a filling breakfast packed with protein like Savory Yogurt Bowl with Chickpeas, Cucumber, and Beets (page 64) or Savory Oatmeal with Poached Egg, Parmesan, and Bacon (page 73); and I always have healthy energy-boosting snacks like Jicama with Chile, Salt, and Lime (page 99) or Vanilla Bean and Espresso Granola (page 84) on hand for hunger attacks. Lunch and dinner change all the time—from fish tacos or fish steamed in parchment to roasted chicken with quinoa—but always feature tons of fresh produce and primarily lean proteins and whole grains—and FLAVOR. I still eat everything I want to; I'm just careful about how much I eat and when I eat.

I also started running seriously again, just as I did in high school when I was on the track team. I lace up my sneakers every morning, rain or shine—even when I'm traveling or filming or am dying to hit that snooze button—and get in some miles. It's excellent physical exercise, of course, but it also helps me clear my head and get focused for the day.

There are no magic bullets, no quick fixes. Getting to a place where you feel healthy and energetic can take a while. It can be even harder to maintain that state once you get there. But changes to the way you eat and live can help. Being fit is just as much mental as it is physical.

I am proud to say that I have stuck to this new fit way of life for ten years; I'm healthier now, in my fifties, than I was when I was younger. Sure, there are days when I'd like to walk away from my life in New York City and spend the rest of my life in Italy eating bowls of pasta and gelato until I burst. But nothing good comes without hard work; and staying fit requires no less effort than running a business or writing a cookbook or taping a cooking show. You have to give it your all.

One of our responsibilities to ourselves is to take care of our bodies, inside and out. If we don't take care of ourselves, then we can't take care of others. We have to take charge of our own happiness and healthfulness, and one way that I personally achieve a joyful existence is through healthy eating and exercise.

Healthy Eating Tips

- Eat. Real. Food. That means real, unprocessed, natural ingredients: fruit, vegetables, fish, meat, eggs, whole grains, good fats. A serving of oatmeal is better for you than a slice of bread, even whole-wheat. The oatmeal has been hulled and perhaps rolled, but the wheat in the bread has been hulled, milled, mixed with other ingredients, baked, etc. Don't even get me started on some of the shelf-stable baked goods you can buy in supermarkets these days. Ever try to read the ingredient list? It might be dozens of lines long with things you can't pronounce. Try to eat ingredients as close to their natural state as possible.

- Eating protein at each meal can help you feel fuller longer. Protein comes in many forms be-

sides just meat. Think: Greek yogurt, fish, eggs, cheese, nuts, legumes, and ancient grains.

- Foods rich in soluble and insoluble fiber keep you fuller longer than low-fiber foods and generally tend to be lower in calories. Fiber-rich foods include vegetables, fruits, legumes, and whole grains.

- Vegetables and fish definitely make up more of my diet than ever before. They are what I crave, what I love to cook these days.

- That said, I believe in everything in moderation. I own a Bobby Flay Steak and dozens of Bobby's Burger Palaces, and I still love a great steak and a great burger. When I know I am going to a steakhouse for dinner or to the BBP, it is my only big meal of the day and I try to add a little extra exercise to my routine.

- Fat is not the enemy. I remember when everyone thought you were supposed to eat low-fat everything and carbs were just fine. It turns out that fat should not be eliminated from your diet, especially not good-for-you unsaturated ones like olive oil, avocados, coconut oil, and almonds. There's always some new fad diet. Don't believe the hype.

- Don't swear off alcohol or sweets or bread or whatever. (Especially don't swear off ice cream; that's too cruel.) You'll be miserable— you also may end up going hog wild the next time someone puts a dessert in front of you, eat too much of it, feel bad, and then swear off all sweets again until the cycle repeats itself. I eat a scoop or two of ice cream every week because I love it so much. I buy the best I can find, I eat it slowly, and I truly savor it.

- Make your food tasty and crunchy and crave-worthy and delicious. There is no need to deprive yourself of flavor or texture! Check out the Healthy Basics chapter (page 15) to get started.

- Unless I am working in the kitchen and absolutely need to be tasting, I try never to eat after eight P.M. I just feel better not eating late at night, and I know that since I stopped eating at midnight (which most chefs do), I have definitely lost weight.

- Keep weeknight drinking to a minimum. Alcohol is full of empty calories. That pretty-in-pink Cosmopolitan contains 220 calories per 4-ounce glass. And if you get smashed on Tuesday, you're less likely to get up in time for your seven thirty A.M. fitness class on Wednesday or even Thursday. Drinking on weeknights adds a lot of calories to your week and can really sap your energy level for the rest of the week, especially if you don't have time to make up for lost sleep.

- Staying hydrated is really important for being fit and healthy. Flushing your body with a lot of water helps expel toxins. Experts recommend at least 64 ounces of water a day, especially if you are active. I have so many friends who simply can't stand the "taste" of water so they don't drink it. Not good. If you are one of those people, make or buy infused waters: Add citrus, berries, cucumber, or mint or other herbs to your water to suit your taste.

Fitness Tips

- Start small and be realistic. There is no easy way to get into shape and stay in shape. Set manageable goals. Change one or two things each week.

- Exercise even if you only have fifteen minutes to do it. Really. It's better than nothing and skipping a day can quickly mean skipping a day or two or three. . . . Stay active.

- If you hate to run, don't jump on the treadmill. There are so many fun ways to stay in shape these days: there are boot camps, rowing classes, spinning classes, boxing, ballet barre. Try everything until you find your favorite. If you aren't a gym person, then go for a hike outside. Create your own boot camp at your local park. Jump rope in your backyard.

- Once you've hit a groove, mix things up. Not only can doing the same thing day in and day out get boring, but your body needs to be challenged in new ways or it can become used to a workout. There's no better feeling than being sore from a new workout and knowing you're flexing new muscles.

- Invest in a fitness tracker. They're not cheap (plan to spend $100 or more), but they really do make you walk more, especially if you're the type of person motivated by goals.

- Enlist a friend. You're less likely to bail on a morning run if you know your best friend is waiting for you at the park.

- If you have never worked out in your life or really do feel like you are clueless when it comes to a fitness routine, spend some money on a trainer. When you join a gym, you typically get one free training session. Use it! And if you like it, maybe pay for a few more and have the trainer create a fitness plan for you that includes both cardio and weight training. I have used a trainer on and off for years and I always learn something new and always consider it money well spent.

- Fuel your body before and after working out. A banana or smoothie or a handful of granola gets me going in the morning before I run or hit the gym. I try to eat within an hour of working out and I aim for a balance of protein, carbs, and fat.

HEALTHY BASICS

I am sharing all of my top flavor-building tips and techniques so that you can put together a properly cooked, healthy, tasty meal any time. This is the way I like to eat.

Vinaigrettes

Vinaigrettes are one of the easiest, quickest ways to get tons of flavor into anything—not just salads. And you should definitely make your own; bottled varieties often contain sugar and stabilizers that make them sweet and gloppy.

The classic French-kitchen ratio calls for three parts oil to one part acid. I like my dressing a bit more acidic and so my ratio is almost always two parts oil to one part acid. The acid can be red, white, or rice wine vinegar; sherry, balsamic, or cider vinegar; or lemon, lime, or orange juice; and the oil can be canola, vegetable, regular (sometimes labeled "pure") olive oil, or extra-virgin olive oil (evoo). For a basic dressing I typically use a blend of canola and evoo; for vinaigrettes that I use to finish off a dish, I tend to use just evoo.

These dressings will keep for up to one week tightly covered in the refrigerator unless otherwise noted.

Basic Vinaigrette

MAKES ABOUT ¾ CUP

¼ cup acid (see above)

1 teaspoon kosher salt

¼ teaspoon freshly ground black pepper

½ cup oil

PER 2 TABLESPOONS: Calories **169**; Protein **0g**; Carbohydrates **0g**; Dietary Fiber **0g**; Sugar **0g**; Total Fat **19g**; Saturated Fat **3g**

Whisk together the acid, salt, and pepper in a medium bowl until the salt begins to dissolve. Slowly whisk in the oil, drop by drop at first, and continue whisking until emulsified.

To add a touch of sweetness, or balance the acidity, whisk in 1 teaspoon honey, pure maple syrup, or agave at the end.

VARIATIONS

Mustard Vinaigrette

Whisk in 1 heaping teaspoon Dijon mustard with the acid.

Mustard-Herb Vinaigrette

Whisk in 1 heaping teaspoon Dijon mustard and 2 teaspoons finely chopped fresh herbs (such as flat-leaf parsley, tarragon, basil, mint, and/or cilantro) with the acid.

Pomegranate-Mustard Vinaigrette

Whisk in 1 heaping teaspoon Dijon mustard and 2 teaspoons pomegranate molasses with the acid. Calories **171**; Carbohydrates **1g**; Sugar **1g**

Buttermilk Dressing

MAKES ABOUT 1 CUP

1 garlic clove

1 teaspoon kosher salt

½ cup low-fat buttermilk, well shaken

3 tablespoons 2% Greek yogurt

2 tablespoons low-fat mayonnaise

1 tablespoon cider vinegar

½ teaspoon Dijon mustard

Pinch of cayenne powder or a few dashes of Tabasco sauce

Pinch of freshly ground black pepper

PER 2 TABLESPOONS: Calories **20**; Protein **1g**; Carbohydrates **1g**; Dietary Fiber **0g**; Sugar **1g**; Total Fat **1g**; Saturated Fat **0g**

I *love* buttermilk. Don't get me wrong—I'm not looking to drink a glass of it anytime soon; but I love using it to marinate chicken for fried chicken, I think it's the best in waffle and pancake batter, and truly, I can't bake biscuits without it. The stuff is magic. Because its name has the word "butter" in it, people think that it is fattening, when quite the opposite is true. Traditional buttermilk is the liquid that remains after butter is churned. Nowadays you can buy cultured buttermilk, which, despite the butter in its name, is still low in fat and extra-flavorful, making it perfect in this vinaigrette. For the most part, buttermilk dressings get their thick, extra-creamy texture from sour cream and full-fat mayo, but I cut back the calories a bit by swapping them for Greek yogurt and low-fat mayonnaise. This is buttermilk dressing at its most basic, but it easily transforms into Blue Cheese and Green Goddess dressings; see the variations, below.

In a small bowl, mash the garlic to a paste with the salt. Whisk in the buttermilk, yogurt, mayonnaise, vinegar, mustard, cayenne, and black pepper. Cover and refrigerate for at least 1 hour and up to 8 hours to allow the flavors to meld.

VARIATIONS

Blue Cheese Dressing

Stir in 2 tablespoons crumbled blue cheese at the end.

Calories **26**; Total Fat **2g**; Saturated Fat **1g**

Green Goddess Dressing

Add 1 teaspoon each finely chopped fresh flat-leaf parsley, tarragon, chives, and dill.

Carrot-Ginger Vinaigrette

MAKES ABOUT 1½ CUPS

1 cup grated carrot (about 1 medium)

1-inch piece of fresh ginger, peeled and chopped

2 tablespoons white miso

2 tablespoons chopped shallot

¼ cup rice wine vinegar

1 tablespoon low-sodium tamari

Pinch of freshly ground black pepper

½ cup canola oil

PER 2 TABLESPOONS: Calories 96; Protein 1g; Carbohydrates 3g; Dietary Fiber 0g; Sugar 1g; Total Fat 9g; Saturated Fat 1g

This bright vinaigrette is used to dress simple salads at Japanese restaurants across the world. It's equally delicious spooned over fish, seafood, and meat. Carrots and ginger are a given, but the secret ingredient in this dressing is white miso, which can be found in the refrigerated section of your grocery store next to the tofu. White miso, which actually ranges in color from light beige to pale yellow, is the sweetest, mildest type of this protein- and nutrient-packed fermented soybean paste with a salty, umami-rich flavor.

In a blender, combine the carrot, ginger, miso, shallot, vinegar, tamari, pepper, and a few tablespoons of water and blend until the mixture is smooth. With the motor running, slowly add the oil and continue blending until just emulsified. This vinaigrette will keep for 3 days refrigerated.

Nutty Vinaigrette

MAKES ABOUT 1 CUP

2 tablespoons natural nut butter

3 tablespoons rice wine vinegar

Juice of 1 lime

1 tablespoon low-sodium tamari

1 teaspoon toasted sesame oil

⅛ teaspoon honey

Pinch of kosher salt

¼ teaspoon freshly ground black pepper

3 tablespoons canola oil

PER 2 TABLESPOONS: Calories 81; Protein 1g; Carbohydrates 2g; Dietary Fiber 0g; Sugar 1g; Total Fat 8g; Saturated Fat 1g

I love using a nut butter–based vinaigrette on chicken, pork, and shrimp dishes as well as on whole-grain and soba noodle salads with lots of vegetables. Just a few tablespoons of nut butter (peanut, almond, or cashew) add an earthy flavor and creamy texture. Natural nut butters contain no added sugar or preservatives and are recommended for this recipe. If you want your vinaigrette to be a touch smoky or spicy, add a teaspoon of chipotle in adobo puree or a pinch of red pepper flakes.

In a blender, combine the nut butter, vinegar, lime juice, tamari, sesame oil, honey, salt, pepper, and a few tablespoons of water and blend until smooth. With the motor running, slowly add the oil and blend until emulsified.

VARIATION

Cilantro-Peanut Vinaigrette

Use peanut butter, add 2 tablespoons chopped fresh cilantro, and blend until just combined.

Carrot-Ginger
Vinaigrette

Green Goddess
Dressing

Nutty
Vinaigrette

Sauces, Salsas, and Relishes

I have made my living off of these three things, which can take the plainest piece of protein and turn it into a gourmet event. At Mesa Grill nearly every dish is served with one and sometimes two. All are freshly made every day and, for the most part, are really healthy. My training may have been in French (read: butter- and cream-laden) cuisine, but it was in my early days working for Jonathan Waxman that I learned that there are so many other ways to get great flavor and texture to a dish without adding tons of fat and calories. Here are some of my favorite healthy sauces, salsas, and relishes, which go perfectly with beef, chicken, pork, and fish. Mix and match to your heart's delight!

Pico de Gallo

MAKES ABOUT 2 CUPS

½ small red or white onion, finely diced

1¼ pounds tomatoes (beefsteak or plum), seeded and finely diced

1 or 2 serrano or jalapeño peppers, to taste, finely diced

Juice of 2 limes

1½ teaspoons kosher salt

¼ teaspoon freshly ground black pepper

¼ cup coarsely chopped fresh cilantro

PER 2 TABLESPOONS: Calories **10**; Protein **0g**; Carbohydrates **2g**; Dietary Fiber **1g**; Sugar **1g**; Total Fat **0g**; Saturated Fat **0g**

Seriously, this is so easy and delicious that you could never again buy a prepared version from the refrigerated section of your grocery store! I love eating this with Baked Tortilla Chips (page 97), adding a few spoonfuls to scrambled eggs, or using it to top grilled fish or chicken. The key is finding the ripest, freshest tomatoes possible—not always easy, I know, but without a doubt it's worth the search. Soaking the onions in ice water for a bit takes out some of their sharpness and makes them super crunchy.

1. Combine 1 cup ice and 1 cup cold water in a small bowl and let sit for 5 minutes. Remove the ice and discard. Add the onion and let soak for 5 minutes. Drain and pat dry.

2. Put the onion, tomatoes, serrano peppers, lime juice, salt, and black pepper in a large bowl and stir until combined. Add the cilantro, cover, and let sit at room temperature for 30 minutes before serving, or refrigerate for up to 8 hours and bring to room temperature before serving.

Cooked Tomato Salsa

MAKES ABOUT 2 CUPS

3 pounds overly ripe beefsteak tomatoes, seeded and chopped (about 3 large)

1 jalapeño or serrano pepper, chopped

2 garlic cloves, chopped

2 tablespoons canola oil

½ teaspoon ground dried oregano, preferably Mexican

Kosher salt and freshly ground black pepper

PER 2 TABLESPOONS: Calories **34**; Protein **1g**; Carbohydrates **4g**; Dietary Fiber **1g**; Sugar **2g**; Total Fat **2g**; Saturated Fat **0g**

Basically a tomato relish, blended and cooked until thick, this salsa leaves the jarred versions in the dust. So simple and delicious, this is another great sauce to have on hand to wake up grilled meat, fish, and veggies, to drizzle over eggs, or to spoon over tacos. And let's not forget the obvious: As a simple flavorful dip with chips, this salsa can't be beat.

In a blender, combine the tomatoes, jalapeño pepper, and garlic and blend until smooth. Add the oil to a medium, high-sided sauté pan and heat over medium heat until it begins to shimmer. Carefully add the tomato mixture and oregano and cook until the sauce thickens and deepens in color, about 15 minutes. Season with salt and black pepper. Serve hot or at room temperature. Once cool, the sauce will keep covered for 5 days in the refrigerator.

Avocado Crema

MAKES ABOUT 1 CUP

2 medium ripe Hass avocados, peeled, pitted, and chopped

Juice of 2 limes

Kosher salt and freshly ground black pepper

PER 2 TABLESPOONS: Calories **71**; Protein **1g**; Carbohydrates **4g**; Dietary Fiber **2g**; Sugar **0g**; Total Fat **6g**; Saturated Fat **1g**

Relying on the natural rich creaminess of avocados and the power of your blender, this dairy-free crema is perfect for vegans and anyone who loves the pure, clean flavor of this delicious fruit. Use it in place of sour cream on fish tacos or as a dip for crudité.

In a blender, combine the avocados, lime juice, and ¼ cup water and blend until smooth. Season with salt and pepper.

VARIATION

Cilantro-Spice Avocado Crema

Add ½ jalapeño, chopped; ¼ teaspoon ground cumin; ¼ teaspoon ground coriander; and ¼ cup fresh cilantro to the ingredients and blend until smooth.

Pico de Gallo

Muhammara

Avocado Crema

Green Harissa

Mustard-Mint
Glaze

Tzatziki

MAKES ABOUT 1½ CUPS

2 garlic cloves

1 teaspoon kosher salt

1 cup 2% Greek yogurt

½ cup English cucumber, coarsely grated and drained on paper towels

1 teaspoon finely grated lemon zest

Juice of ½ lemon

2 tablespoons finely chopped fresh dill

¼ teaspoon freshly ground black pepper

PER 2 TABLESPOONS: Calories **14**; Protein **1g**; Carbohydrates **1g**; Dietary Fiber **0g**; Sugar **1g**; Total Fat **0g**; Saturated Fat **0g**

Best known as that white yogurt sauce on your gyro, tzatziki is the ranch dressing of Greece, just with a bit more flavor and texture. I love it. I can spoon it over anything—it's amazing with simple Greek taverna–inspired grilled fish and meats, served alongside greens or roasted potatoes, or as a dip for some fresh hot pita or crispy crudités. Made with healthy, nutritious, low-fat (in this case) Greek yogurt and popping with flavor from lemon, herbs, garlic, and cucumber, this sauce tastes fattening while being anything but—a perfect example of why the Mediterranean diet is just so amazing.

In a small bowl, mash the garlic to a paste with the salt. Mix in the yogurt, cucumber, lemon zest, lemon juice, dill, and pepper. Cover and refrigerate for at least 1 hour and up to 24 hours to allow the flavors to meld.

VARIATIONS

Feta Tzatziki

Add ¼ cup crumbled feta at the end. Calories **19**; Protein **2g**; Total Fat **1g**; Saturated Fat **1g**

Radish Tzatziki

Replace the grated cucumber with grated radish.

Cherry Tomato Tzatziki

Add 6 quartered cherry tomatoes. Calories **16**; Carbohydrates **2g**

Herbed Tzatziki

Add other finely chopped fresh herbs, such as flat-leaf parsley, cilantro, or even basil.

Guacamole

MAKES ABOUT 4 CUPS

Kosher salt

1 cup fresh or frozen peas

1 serrano or jalapeño pepper,
  finely diced

¼ cup chopped fresh cilantro

3 ripe Hass avocados, peeled and
  pitted

½ small red onion, finely diced

Juice of 2 limes, to taste

Freshly ground black pepper

Thinly sliced green onion, for garnish
  (optional)

PER 2 TABLESPOONS: Calories **28**;
Protein **1g**; Carbohydrates **2g**;
Dietary Fiber **1g**; Sugar **0g**;
Total Fat **2g**; Saturated Fat **0g**

There may just be a recipe for guacamole in every single one of my cookbooks, and I'm okay with that because it plays a big role in my cooking and in my diet. I love avocados in any shape or form and could literally eat a bowl of guacamole by myself on a daily basis. Avocados are high in fat, but that's the cholesterol-free, "good," heart-healthy monounsaturated type. A great source of B vitamins and a host of other vitamins and minerals, avocados are also full of fiber—and it's that fiber and fat that make avocados (and this guacamole) oh so satisfying. This version incorporates peas for some extra vegetable action and fiber, and because they add a nice touch of sweetness and texture. Adding tart raw tomatillos makes another variation, below, that I just love.

1. Bring a small pot of water to a boil, season with salt, and add the peas. Cook the peas for 2 minutes if fresh and 1 minute if frozen. Drain and run under cold water to cool. Drain again on a plate lined with paper towels.

2. In a food processor, combine ¾ cup of the peas, the serrano pepper, and the cilantro and process until almost smooth but still a bit chunky.

3. Put the avocados in a large bowl and coarsely mash with a fork. Fold in the pea mixture and red onion, add the lime juice, and season with salt and black pepper. Garnish with the reserved whole peas and with sliced green onion, if desired.

VARIATION

Tomatillo Guacamole

Add 2 fresh tomatillos, husked, scrubbed, and finely diced, with the folded ingredients. Calories **29**

Curry Sauce

MAKES ABOUT 2 CUPS

2 tablespoons canola oil

1 small Spanish onion, halved and thinly sliced

2 garlic cloves, finely grated or smashed to a paste

2 tablespoons finely grated peeled fresh ginger

2 tablespoons red, green, or yellow curry paste (or 2 tablespoons mild or hot curry powder)

1 cup Best Vegetable Stock (page 140) or low-sodium store-bought, or water

1 (14-ounce) can low-fat coconut milk

Kosher salt and freshly ground black pepper

Finely grated zest of 1 lime

Juice of 2 limes

PER 2 TABLESPOONS: Calories **38**; Protein **0g**; Carbohydrates **2g**; Dietary Fiber **0g**; Sugar **1g**; Total Fat **3g**; Saturated Fat **1g**

I love curry: red, green, yellow—any and all. Each one is unique. In this case, I'm not talking about the spice jar of yellow powder, but the Thai sauces made from various chile-laden spice pastes. They pair perfectly with fish, poultry, meat, veggies, and rice and/or other grains, and all can pretty much be made with the same method. I substitute low-fat canned coconut milk for the full-fat variety—it is really every bit as delicious. Each spoonful packs a wallop of big, bold flavor to give you one satisfying meal.

1. Heat the oil in a medium saucepan over medium heat until it begins to shimmer. Add the onion and cook until very soft and pale golden in color, about 6 minutes. Add the garlic and ginger and cook for 1 minute.

2. Add the curry paste and cook, stirring constantly, until lightly toasted and deepened in color, about 2 minutes. Stir in the stock and cook until reduced by half, about 5 minutes. Add the coconut milk and bring to a boil. Reduce the heat and simmer, stirring occasionally, until the mixture is thickened and less gritty and the curry flavor has mellowed, about 30 minutes.

3. Transfer to a blender and blend until smooth. Season with salt and pepper, add the lime zest and juice, and blend for a few more seconds. Use immediately or let cool and then cover and refrigerate for up to 2 days.

VARIATIONS

Peanut Red Curry Sauce

Whisk in 2 tablespoons natural peanut butter before blending and cook for 1 minute. Calories **51**; Protein **1g**; Total Fat **4g**; Saturated Fat **2g**

Pepper Curry Sauce

Halve, seed, and thinly slice 2 small bell peppers, 1 red and 1 yellow, and cook with the onion until soft. Calories **41**

Green Herb Green Curry Sauce

Add 2 tablespoons each of chopped fresh cilantro and Thai basil at the end.

Muhammara

1 pound red bell peppers

1 or 2 small hot red peppers

Canola oil

Kosher salt and ground black pepper

1 cup walnut pieces, toasted

1 large garlic clove, coarsely chopped

2 tablespoons extra-virgin olive oil

1 tablespoon pomegranate molasses

1 tablespoon sherry vinegar

1 teaspoon ground cumin

1 teaspoon smoked paprika

Grated zest and juice of ½ lemon

PER 2 TABLESPOONS: Calories **58**;
Protein **1g**; Carbohydrates **3g**;
Dietary Fiber **1g**; Sugar **1g**;
Total Fat **5g**; Saturated Fat **1g**

This flavorful red pepper and walnut dip is a star of the Middle Eastern mezze platter. Pomegranate molasses adds its signature sweet-and-sour touch and highlights the flavor play between the sweet roasted red peppers and the spicy notes of hot red peppers, smoky spices, and sharp garlic.

1. Preheat the oven to 400°F.

2. Brush the peppers with a little canola oil and season with salt and pepper. Place them on a baking sheet and roast, turning once, until charred on both sides, about 30 minutes. Remove from the oven, transfer to a bowl, cover with plastic wrap, and let steam for 15 minutes before removing the skin and seeds. Coarsely chop the peppers.

3. In a food processor, combine the bell peppers, one of the hot peppers, the walnuts, garlic, olive oil, pomegranate molasses, vinegar, cumin, and paprika and process until a smooth paste forms. Season with salt. Taste and add the additional hot pepper if desired. Stir in the lemon zest and juice by hand. If the mixture is too thick, drizzle in a little water. Serve immediately or cover and refrigerate for up to 1 day.

Mustard-Mint Glaze

¼ cup Dijon mustard

2 tablespoons whole-grain mustard

2 tablespoons prepared horseradish, drained

1 tablespoon honey

2 tablespoons finely chopped mint

Kosher salt and ground black pepper

PER TABLESPOON: Calories **16**;
Protein **0g**; Carbohydrates **3g**;
Dietary Fiber **0g**; Sugar **2g**;
Total Fat **0g**; Saturated Fat **0g**

An incredibly versatile glaze, this blend of mustards, honey, horseradish, and mint is as delicious on a lean steak as it is salmon or even shellfish. Chicken breasts are a given and lamb makes for a particularly classic pairing.

In a small bowl, whisk together the mustards, horseradish, honey, mint, and salt and pepper to taste. Cover and let sit for at least 30 minutes to allow the flavors to meld.

Ancho Honey Glaze

MAKES ½ CUP

½ cup honey

1 heaping tablespoon ancho chile powder (or any pure chile powder)

Kosher salt and ground black pepper

PER TABLESPOON: Calories **69**; Protein **0g**; Carbohydrates **17g**; Dietary Fiber **0g**; Sugar **17g**; Total Fat **0g**; Saturated Fat **0g**

This glaze couldn't be any simpler, but that doesn't mean it's not powerful. The one-two sweet-and-spicy punch of flavor is delicious on pork and chicken, and I'm particularly fond of using it to glaze salmon fillets.

In a medium bowl, whisk together the honey, chile powder, salt, and pepper. Cover and let sit for 15 minutes before using.

Green Harissa

MAKES ABOUT 2 CUPS

1 teaspoon coriander seed, toasted (see Note) and ground

1 teaspoon fennel seed, toasted and ground

1 teaspoon cumin seed, toasted and ground

1 teaspoon caraway seed, toasted and ground

1 poblano pepper, roasted (see page 27), peeled, and seeded

3 serrano peppers, seeded

2 garlic cloves

1 cup fresh flat-leaf parsley

1 cup fresh cilantro

½ cup fresh mint

Kosher salt and ground black pepper

½ cup extra-virgin olive oil

PER TABLESPOON: Calories **41**; Protein **0g**; Carbohydrates **1g**; Dietary Fiber **0g**; Sugar **0g**; Total Fat **4g**; Saturated Fat **1g**

I love red harissa paste (made with red chiles) and use it often at my restaurant Gato. But there's no reason red chiles should have all the fun. This version is made with the same dried spices as the original, but with green chiles in place of the red and lots of green herbs that give the harissa a fresh taste. Great served on meats, fish, and poultry, it's also excellent swirled into dips like hummus and guacamole, giving them new life with its punch of heat and freshness.

In a food processor, combine all of the ingredients and pulse to combine. Process until thoroughly pureed to a paste-like consistency, adding a few tablespoons of water if needed. Be careful not to overprocess or the greens will start to blacken. Store in a container with a tight-fitting lid and refrigerate until ready to use or for up to 1 week.

NOTE

To toast spices: Put the spices in a dry sauté pan over medium heat and cook, tossing constantly, until just fragrant, about 3 minutes. Let cool completely.

Roasted Red Pepper Tomato Sauce

MAKES ABOUT 4 CUPS

2 tablespoons olive oil

1 large yellow onion, coarsely chopped

4 garlic cloves, coarsely chopped

¼ teaspoon red pepper flakes, preferably Calabrian

4 jarred roasted red bell peppers, drained, patted dry, and chopped

2 (28-ounce) cans plum tomatoes and juices, crushed with your hands

¼ cup chopped fresh flat-leaf parsley

3 tablespoons finely chopped fresh basil

1 tablespoon finely chopped fresh oregano

Kosher salt and freshly ground black pepper

PER ½ CUP: Calories **64**; Protein **1g**; Carbohydrates **7g**; Dietary Fiber **2g**; Sugar **4g**; Total Fat **4g**; Saturated Fat **1g**

Yes, you could roast your own, but this sauce makes the most of the pantry staple, roasted red peppers. Sweet and smoky, they get a kick from Calabrian chile flakes; freshness from parsley, basil, and oregano; and of course, the savory depth from onion and garlic, the base of many good things. Cooked with canned plum tomatoes until thick and sweet, this bright red sauce is one I turn to all the time.

1. In a large Dutch oven, heat the oil over medium-high heat until it shimmers. Add the onion and cook until soft, about 5 minutes. Add the garlic and red pepper flakes and cook for 1 minute. Add the roasted red peppers and cook for 1 minute.

2. Add the tomatoes, bring to a boil, and cook, stirring occasionally, until the sauce has thickened and reduced by half, about 30 minutes.

3. Transfer the mixture to a food processor and process until smooth. Return the mixture to the pot, add the parsley, basil, and oregano, and season with salt and pepper. Simmer over low heat for 10 minutes. Use immediately or let cool and then cover and refrigerate for up to 2 days.

**Pickled Saffron
Shallots**

Pickled Beets (Red)

Pickles

Pickled vegetables add great crunch and acid to dishes, and they are a tasty, fat-free, low-calorie snack. The sky is the limit when it comes to veggies as are the vinegar, sweetener, and spices that you use. (And if you have never had pickled hard-cooked eggs, definitely try those, too; see page 115.) The brines also make a great base for vinaigrettes.

Pickled Chiles

Pickled Radishes

**Pickled Beets
(Yellow)**

Pickled Chiles

MAKES 1 CUP

6 ounces fresno or jalapeño peppers
(about 8 medium), sliced crosswise
into rings

1 garlic clove, crushed

1 teaspoon mustard seeds

1 teaspoon coriander seeds

¼ teaspoon whole black
peppercorns

1¼ cups white wine vinegar

3 tablespoons sugar

2 tablespoons kosher salt

PER DRAINED ¼ CUP: Calories 16;
Protein 1g; Carbohydrates 3g;
Dietary Fiber 1g; Sugar 1g;
Total Fat 0g; Saturated Fat 0g

These are perfect on tacos, a must on nachos, and an excellent accompaniment to just about any Mexican or Southwestern dish.

1. Put the peppers and garlic in a heat-proof 2-quart or larger jar with a lid.

2. In a small nonreactive saucepan, toast the mustard seeds, coriander seeds, and peppercorns over medium-low heat, stirring, until fragrant, about 2 minutes. Add the vinegar, sugar, salt, and 1 cup water and bring to a simmer. Cook until the sugar and salt have dissolved, about 4 minutes.

3. Pour the hot brine over the peppers and garlic and let cool to room temperature, about 2 hours. Cover and refrigerate for at least 4 hours and up to 2 weeks.

Pickled Red Onions

MAKES ABOUT 2 CUPS

1½ cups fresh lime juice

2 tablespoons sugar

1 tablespoon kosher salt

5 fresh cilantro sprigs (without the
leaves)

1 large onion, halved and thinly
sliced

PER DRAINED ¼ CUP: Calories 9;
Protein 0g; Carbohydrates 2g;
Dietary Fiber 0g; Sugar 2g;
Total Fat 0g; Saturated Fat 0g

I add these beauties (they turn such a gorgeous magenta hue) to dishes across the spectrum—any time I want to add a little pep. They also have become one of my favorite burger toppings.

1. In a small nonreactive saucepan, combine 1 cup water, the juice, sugar, and salt, bring to a boil, and cook until the sugar and salt dissolve, about 2 minutes. Remove from the heat, add the cilantro stems, and let cool for just 10 minutes.

2. Put the onion in a heat-proof 2-quart or larger jar with a lid. Pour the warm brine over the onion, cover, and refrigerate for at least 4 hours and up to 2 weeks. Remove the cilantro stems before serving.

Pickled Beets

MAKES 2 QUARTS

1 pound beets, red or yellow, scrubbed and stems trimmed

1 tablespoon canola oil

Kosher salt and freshly ground black pepper

3 cups cider vinegar

¼ cup sugar

1 large shallot, halved and thinly sliced

8 whole black peppercorns

6 whole cloves

PER DRAINED ¼ CUP: Calories **12**; Protein **0g**; Carbohydrates **2g**; Dietary Fiber **0g**; Sugar **1g**; Total Fat **0g**; Saturated Fat **0g**

Earthy beets are transformed when pickled; their natural sweetness meets its match in acidic cider vinegar, and cloves, peppercorns, and shallots ensure that these beets are savory, bar none.

1. Preheat the oven to 400°F.

2. Rub the beets with the oil and season with salt and pepper. Wrap individually in foil, put on a baking sheet, and roast until a skewer inserted into the center meets with no resistance, 50 to 75 minutes. Let cool, then peel, and cut into 1-inch dice. Transfer to a heat-proof 2-quart or larger jar with a lid.

3. In a nonreactive saucepan, combine the vinegar, 2 cups water, the sugar, 2 tablespoons salt, the shallot, peppercorns, and cloves, bring to a boil, and cook until the sugar and salt have dissolved, about 2 minutes. Remove from the heat and let cool for 5 minutes. Pour over the beets, cover, and refrigerate for at least 8 hours and up to 3 days.

Pickled Radishes

MAKES 1 PINT

3 cups rice wine vinegar

¼ cup sugar

2 tablespoons kosher salt

10 whole yellow mustard seeds

Small bunch of fresh dill, coarsely chopped

1 pint small mixed radishes, with greens, if possible, trimmed

PER DRAINED ¼ CUP: Calories **8**; Protein **0g**; Carbohydrates **2g**; Dietary Fiber **0g**; Sugar **1g**; Total Fat **0g**; Saturated Fat **0g**

I prefer the mild nature of rice wine vinegar when pickling radishes as it really allows their peppery bite to shine through. Keep the greens, if you can find them, in a good-looking bunch. Gotta love the built-in handle!

1. In a nonreactive saucepan, combine the vinegar, 2 cups water, the sugar, salt, and mustard seeds, bring to a boil, and cook until the sugar and salt have dissolved, about 2 minutes. Remove from the heat and add the dill. Let cool for 5 minutes.

2. Put the radishes in a heat-proof 2-quart or larger jar with a lid. Pour the brine over them, cover, and refrigerate for at least 8 hours and up to 3 days.

Pickled Green Onions

MAKES ABOUT 2 CUPS

2 cups cider vinegar

2 tablespoons sugar

1 tablespoon kosher salt

1 jalapeño pepper, seeded and chopped

1 garlic clove, peeled and sliced

½ teaspoon coriander seeds

1 bunch of green onions, trimmed and halved lengthwise

PER DRAINED ¼ CUP: Calories **9**; Protein **0g**; Carbohydrates **2g**; Dietary Fiber **1g**; Sugar **1g**; Total Fat **0g**; Saturated Fat **0g**

Green onions may look delicate, but they really do have quite a pungent oniony bite. Pickling mellows that, but tossing jalapeño and garlic into the brine ensures that these pickles are anything but humdrum.

1. In a medium nonreactive saucepan, combine the vinegar, ¾ cup water, the sugar, salt, jalapeño, garlic, and coriander seeds, bring to a boil, and cook until the sugar and salt have dissolved, 2 minutes. Remove from the heat and let cool to room temperature, about 15 minutes.

2. Put the green onions in a heat-proof 2-quart or larger jar with a lid. Pour the brine over them, cover, and refrigerate for at least 2 hours and up to 2 days.

Pickled Saffron Shallots

MAKES ABOUT 1½ CUPS

1½ cups white wine vinegar

2 tablespoons sugar

1 tablespoon kosher salt

Pinch of saffron

1 garlic clove, smashed

1 teaspoon whole black peppercorns

1 teaspoon whole fennel seeds

6 large shallots, thinly sliced

PER DRAINED ¼ CUP: Calories **32**; Protein **1g**; Carbohydrates **7g**; Dietary Fiber **1g**; Sugar **4g**; Total Fat **0g**; Saturated Fat **0g**

The saffron infuses these shallots with a bright color and a Mediterranean flavor. They are wonderful on burgers and sandwiches or with seafood dishes like Cod in Spicy Ginger Broth with Mushrooms and Cockles (page 177).

1. In a small nonreactive saucepan, bring 1 cup water, the vinegar, sugar, salt, saffron, garlic, peppercorns, and fennel seeds to a boil and cook until the sugar and salt dissolve, about 2 minutes. Remove from the heat and let cool for 10 minutes.

2. Put the shallots in a heat-proof 2-quart or larger jar with a lid. Pour the warm brine over them, cover, and refrigerate for at least 2 hours and up to 2 days. Remove the garlic and spices before serving.

Spice Rubs

Spice rubs are a really easy way to add complex flavor and incredible texture to meat, chicken, fish, and even vegetables, without adding extra fat and calories. The sky is the limit when it comes to flavor combinations, and making spice rubs is a great way to use up all of those bottles in your pantry before they expire. These rubs will keep, covered tightly and stored in a cabinet, for six months.

Mediterranean Spice Rub

MAKES ABOUT ½ CUP

2 tablespoons fennel seed

2 tablespoons coriander seed

1 tablespoon mustard seed

1 tablespoon cumin seed

2 teaspoons ground turmeric

½ teaspoon cayenne powder

1 tablespoon brown sugar

1 tablespoon kosher salt

½ tablespoon freshly ground black pepper

PER TEASPOON: Calories **8**; Protein **0g**; Carbohydrates **1g**; Dietary Fiber **1g**; Sugar **0g**; Total Fat **0g**; Saturated Fat **0g**

This combination of spices is particularly good on fish, lamb, and chicken.

1. In a small, dry sauté pan, combine the fennel seed, coriander seed, mustard seed, and cumin seed and toast the spices over medium heat until fragrant, about 3 minutes. Remove the spices from the pan and let cool. Grind to a fine powder in a spice grinder or with a mortar and pestle.

2. In a small bowl, combine the toasted spices with the turmeric, cayenne, brown sugar, salt, and pepper and stir until thoroughly mixed.

Adobo Seasoning

MAKES ABOUT ⅔ CUP

¼ cup kosher salt

1 heaping tablespoon granulated garlic

1 heaping tablespoon granulated onion

1 heaping tablespoon ground turmeric

1 heaping tablespoon freshly ground black pepper

2 teaspoons ground cumin

2 teaspoons sweet Spanish paprika

1 tablespoon finely chopped fresh oregano

PER TEASPOON: Calories **2**; Protein **0g**; Carbohydrates **0g**; Dietary Fiber **0g**; Sugar **0g**; Total Fat **0g**; Saturated Fat **0g**

This savory, garlicky spice mixture is essential to Spanish, Caribbean, and Latin American cooking. Used to season fish, chicken, meat, or rice, this mix is truly all-purpose.

In a small bowl, mix together the salt, granulated garlic, granulated onion, turmeric, black pepper, cumin, paprika, and oregano.

Spanish Spice Rub

MAKES ABOUT ½ CUP

¼ cup sweet Spanish paprika

1½ tablespoons ground cumin

1½ tablespoons dry mustard powder

1 tablespoon ground fennel

1 teaspoon kosher salt

1 teaspoon coarsely ground black pepper

PER TEASPOON: Calories **9**; Protein **0g**; Carbohydrates **1g**; Dietary Fiber **1g**; Sugar **0g**; Total Fat **0g**; Saturated Fat **0g**

This rub is great for pork, steak, chicken, and fish. For extra flavor, let the rubbed meat or fish sit for fifteen minutes before cooking.

In a small bowl, mix together the paprika, cumin, mustard, fennel, salt, and pepper.

Steak Rub

MAKES ABOUT 1 CUP

¼ cup ancho chile powder

2 tablespoons sweet Spanish paprika

2 tablespoons ground cumin

2 tablespoons ground coriander

2 tablespoons dry mustard powder

2 tablespoons dried oregano

1 tablespoon kosher salt

2 teaspoons freshly ground black pepper

1 teaspoon cayenne powder

PER TEASPOON: Calories **8**; Protein **0g**; Carbohydrates **1g**; Dietary Fiber **1g**; Sugar **0g**; Total Fat **0g**; Saturated Fat **0g**

This is my go-to rub for steak and pork. It made its debut many years ago on Mesa Grill New York's menu and it always satisfies. Make extra and keep it tightly covered in a cool, dark place so you always have it on hand.

In a small bowl, stir together all of the spices.

Frico

Quinoa Croutons

Baked Tofu
Croutons

Crunch

Contrast of texture is just as important as flavor in a dish. I love crunch, whether from a tortilla chip alongside a creamy guacamole, the crust of perfectly fried chicken, or the caramelized topping of a smooth-as-silk crème brûlée. Crunch is even more important when it comes to healthier foods where fat is lower and portions are smaller. You are left wanting a bit more and that is where crunch comes in, providing additional texture and interest. These crunchy recipes are filled with protein and fiber, are so easy to make, and can be eaten as is or used to enliven other recipes.

Crispy Whole-Wheat Couscous

MAKES 1 CUP

¼ teaspoon kosher salt

⅛ teaspoon freshly ground black pepper

½ cup whole-wheat couscous

2 tablespoons olive oil

PER TABLESPOON: Calories **42**; Protein **1g**; Carbohydrates **6g**; Dietary Fiber **1g**; Sugar **0g**; Total Fat **2g**; Saturated Fat **0g**

Steamed then crisped in a touch of oil, whole-wheat couscous becomes akin to toasted bread crumbs in no time at all, and creates a toasty, crunchy garnish for all kinds of dishes.

1. Bring ½ cup water to a boil in a small saucepan and add the salt and pepper. Put the couscous in a small heat-proof bowl, add the boiling water, and stir to combine. Cover and let sit for 5 minutes. Fluff with a fork.

2. Heat the oil in a medium nonstick sauté pan until it begins to shimmer. Add the couscous and press into an even layer on the bottom of the pan. Cook, stirring with a fork to keep it separate, until golden brown and crisp, about 5 minutes. Use immediately or let cool, cover, and store for up to 1 day. Re-crisp in a dry nonstick pan before using.

Quinoa Croutons

MAKES 24 CROUTONS

Nonstick cooking spray

1 cup old-fashioned rolled oats, such as Bob's Red Mill

½ cup quinoa

½ cup slivered almonds

½ cup pumpkin seeds

¼ cup coconut oil, melted; canola oil; or a combination

1 tablespoon honey, pure maple syrup, or agave syrup

1 teaspoon smoked paprika or chile powder

1 teaspoon kosher salt

¼ teaspoon freshly ground black pepper

PER SERVING (3 CROUTONS):
Calories **211**; Protein **5g**; Carbohydrates **21g**; Dietary Fiber **3g**; Sugar **3g**; Total Fat **12g**; Saturated Fat **6g**

Whether it's a tossed salad of tender greens or a bowl of creamy oats, adding an element of crunch is essential. These nutty seeded croutons of hearty oats and toasty quinoa do just the trick—and an extra squeeze of honey and replacing the paprika with dried fruit transforms these from savory to sweet in an instant.

1. Preheat the oven to 300°F. Line a 9 × 13-inch rimmed baking sheet with parchment paper and spray with nonstick spray.

2. In a large bowl, toss the oats with the quinoa, almonds, and pumpkin seeds to combine. Whisk together the coconut oil, honey, paprika, salt, and pepper in a small bowl. Add the oil mixture to the oat mixture and toss until it forms clumps.

3. Spread the mixture onto the prepared baking sheet in a thin, even layer. Bake on the middle oven rack until light golden brown and crispy, about 25 minutes.

4. Remove the pan to a baking rack and let cool completely. Break into clusters or cut into crouton shapes.

VARIATION

Sweetened Quinoa Croutons

Omit the paprika and increase the honey, maple syrup, or agave syrup to 3 tablespoons. Stir in ½ cup chopped unsweetened dried cherries or cranberries once cool.

Calories **260**; Carbohydrates **32g**; Sugar **10g**

Baked Tofu Croutons

MAKES 24 CROUTONS

16 ounces extra-firm tofu

1 tablespoon toasted sesame oil

1 tablespoon soy sauce

1 tablespoon rice vinegar

Optional additions

1 tablespoon finely chopped garlic

¼ teaspoon red pepper flakes,
   preferably Calabrian

Few dashes of hot sauce

1 teaspoon chile-garlic paste

2 tablespoons barbecue sauce

PER SERVING (3 CROUTONS):
Calories **75**; Protein **7g**;
Carbohydrates **1g**; Dietary Fiber **1g**;
Sugar **0g**; Total Fat **5g**; Saturated
Fat **1g**

Excellent for salads, soups, or just eating as a snack, these "croutons" are low in fat and full of protein. I happen to think that the best thing about tofu is how it's a blank canvas for flavor, a sponge to soak up whatever you add to it. Here are the basic recipe and a few suggestions for flavors, but know that you can season the tofu in any way that you want, depending upon what you are pairing it with.

1. Remove the tofu from its packaging and pat dry with paper towels. Line a plate with a paper towel and set the tofu on top. Set a small plate on top of the tofu and weight it down with something heavy, like a 28-ounce can of tomatoes. Press for 15 to 30 minutes. You will see liquid collect around the tofu.

2. Transfer the tofu to a cutting board and slice in half horizontally and then cut lengthwise into 3 strips and then crosswise 4 times. You will have 24 (1-inch) dice.

3. In a medium bowl, whisk together the sesame oil, soy sauce, vinegar, 1 tablespoon water, and other flavorings, if using. Add the tofu and toss until each piece is coated. Cover and let marinate in the refrigerator for at least 30 minutes and up to 4 hours, stirring occasionally.

4. Preheat the oven to 350°F.

5. Line a rimmed baking sheet with parchment paper. Spread the tofu out in an even layer on the baking sheet and bake, turning several times, until golden brown and puffed, about 30 minutes. Serve right away or allow to cool to room temperature before transferring to a container with a lid and refrigerating for up to 1 week.

Frico

MAKES 12

12 ounces finely grated cheese (such as sharp cheddar, Manchego, Romano, Parmigiano-Reggiano, Asiago, or Gruyère)

PER FRICO: Calories **113**; Protein **7g**; Carbohydrates **1g**; Dietary Fiber **0g**; Sugar **0g**; Total Fat **9g**; Saturated Fat **5g**

This light, crispy, cheesy Italian cracker packs a punch of flavor in every bite but is so much less fattening than eating a ton of cheese and crackers. It's a one-ingredient wonder you can eat straight up, topped with relish or tapenade, or as a garnish on a salad or soup. I've included some of my favorite optional additions below to mix things up. Just make sure you start with a cheese that's sharp in flavor and dry in texture.

1. Preheat the oven to 400°F. Line a baking sheet with a silicone baking mat or use a nonstick baking sheet.

2. Put ¼ cup mounds of the cheese onto the prepared pan, spacing each mound ½ inch apart. Bake until flat, lightly golden brown, and crisp, about 5 minutes. Let cool on the sheet for 5 minutes. Transfer to a plate with a metal spatula and allow them to cool completely.

VARIATIONS

Sesame Frico

Add ¼ teaspoon sesame seeds to the cheese.

Fines Herbes Frico

Add 1 teaspoon each finely chopped fresh flat-leaf parsley, tarragon, and chives to the cheese.

Manchego–Smoked Paprika Frico

Add 1 tablespoon smoked paprika to Manchego cheese.

Spiced Almonds

MAKES 1 CUP

1 cup slivered almonds

1 tablespoon honey

1 tablespoon olive oil

1 tablespoon spice rub
 (see pages 35–37)

PER TABLESPOON: Calories **65**;
Protein **2g**; Carbohydrates **3g**;
Dietary Fiber **1g**; Sugar **1g**;
Total Fat **5g**; Saturated Fat **0g**

This makes a quick, nutritious snack that doubles as a topping for salads. Flavor them with any spice rub you like.

1. Preheat the oven to 325°F. Line a rimmed baking sheet with a silicone baking mat or use a nonstick baking sheet.

2. Spread out the almonds in a single layer on the baking sheet and toast in the oven until lightly golden brown, approximately 5 minutes. Let cool slightly.

3. In a large sauté pan over low heat, combine the honey, 1 tablespoon water, the olive oil, and spice rub and heat just until they combine and the spices bloom, about 2 minutes. Off the heat, add the toasted almonds to the pan and toss until they are coated with the honey mixture. Return the almonds to the baking sheet, return to the oven, and bake for 5 minutes longer. Remove and let cool before separating into pieces.

Rice, Grains, and Beans

I am not sure when America's love affair with ancient grains began. Years ago, I served a lamb dish with farro at my restaurant Bolo and 99 percent of the people who ordered it had no idea what it was. Today, many more people have heard of farro—not to mention quinoa, spelt, and wheat berries. These ancient grains have stayed around for good reason: They are delicious and packed with protein, fiber, and nutrients. If you haven't tried them yet, use this quick guide to get familiar with the most popular. Make a batch on Sunday and find ways to use it throughout the week. (I will help you with that, too!)

Wheat Berries

Quinoa

Beans

Pearl Barley

Wild Rice

Brown Rice

Farro

Quinoa

1 CUP DRY = ABOUT 3 CUPS COOKED

Use a ratio of 1 cup quinoa to 2 cups liquid. Combine the quinoa and liquid in a medium saucepan. Season with kosher salt and bring to a boil. Reduce the heat to low, cover, and simmer until the quinoa is tender and most of the liquid has been absorbed, 15 to 20 minutes. Transfer to a bowl and fluff with a fork.

Farro

1 CUP DRY = ABOUT 3 CUPS COOKED

Put the farro in a saucepan and add enough water or stock to cover by 1 inch. Season with kosher salt and bring to a boil. Reduce the heat to medium-low and simmer until tender, about 30 minutes. Drain off any excess liquid.

Brown Rice

1 CUP DRY = ABOUT 3 CUPS COOKED

Most directions say to use a 2:1 ratio of water or stock to rice, brown or white, but in my experience, that ratio produces mushy rice. I prefer 1¾ cups liquid to 1 cup rice. Also, remember to season the liquid: I use 1 teaspoon kosher salt and ¼ teaspoon black pepper per cup of rice.

Combine the liquid, salt, and pepper in a saucepan over high heat, stir in the rice, and bring to a boil. Cover the pan, reduce the heat to medium-low, and simmer until the liquid is absorbed and the rice is perfectly cooked, about 30 minutes. Let the cooked rice sit for 10 minutes, covered, then remove the lid and fluff the grains with a fork.

Wild Rice

1 CUP DRY = ABOUT 3 CUPS COOKED

I love the nutty taste and toothsome chew of wild rice. I fold it into pancakes and tamales and dressings for Thanksgiving. I prefer my rice "overcooked," if you will—totally bloomed. If the taste is too earthy for you, try cutting it with cooked brown rice or quinoa. Use a ratio of 3 cups liquid to 1 cup rice, 1 teaspoon kosher salt, and ¼ teaspoon freshly ground black pepper.

Bring the liquid to a boil, add the salt and pepper, and stir in the wild rice. Cover the pan, reduce the heat to medium-low, and simmer until the liquid is absorbed and the rice kernels open and flower completely, 40 to 45 minutes. Remove the lid and simmer for an additional 5 minutes to dry out the rice. Drain off any excess liquid.

Wheat Berries

1 CUP DRY = ABOUT 3½ CUPS COOKED

Put the wheat berries in a saucepan and add enough water or stock to cover by 2 inches. Season with kosher salt and bring to a boil. Reduce the heat to medium-low and simmer until tender, about 1 hour. Drain off any excess liquid.

Pearl Barley

1 CUP DRY = ABOUT 3½ CUPS COOKED

Rinse the barley in a colander. Put the barley in a saucepan and add enough water or stock to cover by 1 inch. Season with kosher salt and bring to a boil. Reduce the heat to medium-low and simmer until tender, 25 to 30 minutes. Drain off any excess liquid.

Beans

MAKES 6 TO 7 CUPS

1 pound beans (black, white, kidney, or chickpeas), picked over

1 small Spanish onion, halved

2 garlic cloves, smashed (optional)

4 fresh thyme sprigs (optional)

1 tablespoon kosher salt

½ teaspoon freshly ground black pepper

Beans are a staple in nearly every cuisine and have traditionally been the prime protein source in regions where meat is scarce or expensive. Besides providing protein and fiber, beans are a rich source of calcium, phosphorus, and iron. Best of all, these delicious, nutritious legumes can be used in so many ways—try them in salads and soups, with rice or pasta, or in such varied dishes as Moroccan couscous (chickpeas), Mexican refried beans (pintos), Cajun red beans and rice, Southern succotash (limas), or hummus from the Middle East (chickpeas).

The three most consistently good canned products are tomatoes, pumpkin puree, and beans. When I am making a bean puree or dip (such as hummus), however, I often will take that extra step to cook dried beans from scratch. The flavor is fresher and the consistency creamier.

Everyone has a way of cooking beans: overnight soaking, quick soak, no soak, salt, no salt. There is no one exact recipe because the cooking time depends on the beans themselves. The longer your beans have sat on the shelf in your grocery store, the longer they will take to cook. So, use this recipe as a guide and then cook until the beans are soft.

According to *The Kitchen Companion* by Polly Clingerman, a terrific general handbook that I recommend, 1 pound (about 2 cups) of dried beans makes roughly 6 to 7 cups cooked beans, and one 15-ounce can of cooked beans is roughly 1¾ cups drained.

Beans are best stored in their cooking liquid and drained just before using. Store in sealed containers for up to three days in the refrigerator or for several weeks in the freezer.

1. Put the beans in a large pot with plenty of space for expansion, and cover with at least 2 inches of cold water. Bring to a rolling boil, turn off the heat, and let stand for 1 hour.

2. Drain the beans. Return them to the pot and cover them with at least 2 inches of cold water. Add the onion, garlic and thyme, if using, salt, and pepper. Bring to a boil and then reduce the heat so that the water simmers. Cook until tender, anywhere from 1 hour to 2 hours. Discard the onion, garlic, and thyme before serving.

Meat, Poultry, and Fish

Grains, beans, yogurt, and certain vegetables are all great sources of protein and this book is full of recipes for them. There are more vegetarians and vegans in this country than ever before, and as a chef-restaurateur I know better than most just how this group of people is growing. I now offer more vegetable dishes than I ever have in my thirty-plus years of cooking and that's okay. I like giving my customers what they want and I am all about change.

Personally, I still eat meat and fish, though maybe not as much as I did in the past, when I would have 8-ounce portions several times a day. I now know that a much smaller portion is more than enough, and I make up the balance with grains, vegetables, and legumes; it's a healthier and more interesting way to eat.

Here is how I cook my favorite meats, poultry, and fish.

Pan-Seared or Grilled Strip Steak

If you're a red-meat eater looking for a beef alternative, bison (buffalo) is a great lean option. I love it and I have had occasion to serve it at my restaurants on various menus throughout the years. Bison and beef are both protein-rich foods, and the difference in flavor between the two isn't that dramatic, though bison is much lower in fat. Whichever you prefer, I've got you covered.

To pan-sear: Season the meat on both sides with salt and pepper. Heat a little canola oil in a nonstick pan over high heat until it begins to shimmer. Cook the meat on both sides until golden brown and medium-rare, about 4 minutes per side. Remove to a cutting board and let rest for 5 minutes before slicing.

To grill: Heat a grill to high or a grill pan over high heat until it begins to smoke. Brush both sides of the steak with a little canola oil and season with salt and pepper. Grill until golden brown, a little charred on both sides, and medium-rare, about 4 minutes per side. Remove the steak to a cutting board and let rest for 5 minutes before slicing.

Pan-Seared or Grilled Chicken Breast or Chicken Thighs

Lean chicken breast halves are practically the archetypal healthy-eating protein choice, and the mild white meat is preferred by many, but I'll go on the record to say that I love chicken thighs. They have more flavor and stay so much moister as they cook, with less of a risk of overcooking than the breast. Of course that's because thighs have more natural fat, but . . . everything in moderation!

To pan-sear: Heat a little canola oil in a medium nonstick sauté pan over high heat until it begins to shimmer. Season the chicken on both sides with salt and pepper. Cook the chicken until golden brown on both sides and just cooked through, about 4 minutes per side. Remove to a plate and let rest for 5 minutes before serving.

To grill: Heat a grill to high or a grill pan over high heat until it begins to smoke. Brush both sides of the chicken with a little canola oil and season with salt and pepper. Grill until golden brown on both sides and just cooked through, about 4 minutes per side. Remove to a cutting board and let rest for 5 minutes before serving.

Pan-Seared or Grilled Fish

Fish is a high-protein, low-fat food that provides a range of health benefits. White-fleshed fish, in particular, is lower in fat than any other source of animal protein, and oily fish are high in omega-3 fatty acids, or the "good" fats. Since the human body can't make significant amounts of these essential nutrients, fish are an important part of the diet. Also, fish are low in the "bad" fats commonly found in red meat, called omega-6 fatty acids.

These methods are great for thin, white-fleshed fillets or steaks. Salmon or tuna are best cooked a little less, until medium.

To pan-sear: Heat a little canola oil in a medium nonstick sauté pan over high heat until the oil begins to shimmer. Season the fish on both sides with salt and pepper and cook until golden brown on each side and just cooked through, about 3 minutes per side.

To grill: Heat a grill to high or a grill pan over high heat. Brush the fish on both sides with a little canola oil and season with salt and pepper. Grill until golden brown on each side and just cooked through, about 3 minutes per side.

Pan-Seared or Grilled Shrimp or Scallops

Both shrimp and scallops are good sources of heart-healthy nutrients, including protein and vitamins B_{12} and D. Quick cooking and delicious, they are excellent alternative choices to meat, and lend themselves to many different preparations, including grilling, sautéing, roasting, and steaming.

To pan-sear: Heat a little canola oil in a medium nonstick sauté pan over high heat until it begins to shimmer. Season large shrimp or medium scallops with salt and pepper on both sides. Cook shrimp until lightly golden brown on both sides and just cooked through, about 3 minutes total. Cook scallops until the bottom is golden brown, about 3 minutes, then turn them over, and cook for 1 minute longer.

To grill: Heat a grill to high or a grill pan over high heat. Brush the shellfish with a little canola oil and season with salt and pepper. Grill for 2 minutes on the first side until golden brown and slightly charred, then turn them over, and continue cooking for 1 minute longer or until just cooked through.

BREAKFAST

Vanilla Date Smoothie with Nutmeg and Orange

SERVES 2

1 cup 2% Greek yogurt

1 cup skim milk

1 teaspoon finely grated orange zest

½ cup (packed) pitted Medjool dates (about 4 ounces)

½ teaspoon pure vanilla extract

Pinch of ground nutmeg

2 cups ice cubes

PER SERVING: Calories **305**; Protein **12g**; Carbohydrates **58g**; Dietary Fiber **9g**; Sugar **48g**; Total Fat **3g**; Saturated Fat **2g**

I first had this smoothie a few years ago in Los Angeles. Initially I couldn't quite put my finger on what the flavor was and when they told me it was dates, I thought, of course! Dates are a nutritional powerhouse filled with fiber, magnesium, and potassium, and they add a really nice sweetness to this refreshing smoothie.

In a blender, combine the yogurt, milk, orange zest, dates, vanilla, nutmeg, and ice cubes and blend until smooth. Divide between 2 large glasses.

Easy Being
Green Smoothie

Roasted Peach and
Pistachio Smoothie

Coffee Hazelnut
Smoothie

Vanilla Date Smoothie
with Nutmeg and Orange

Roasted Peach and Pistachio Smoothie

SERVES 2

3 very ripe peaches, pitted and coarsely chopped

¼ teaspoon ground cinnamon

1 cup 2% Greek yogurt

Scant ¼ cup toasted shelled pistachios or 2 tablespoons unsweetened pistachio butter

1 teaspoon finely grated orange zest (optional)

⅛ teaspoon pure vanilla extract

½ cup to 1 cup ice cubes, depending on desired thickness

PER SERVING: Calories **238**; Protein **12g**; Carbohydrates **26g**; Dietary Fiber **5g**; Sugar **20g**; Total Fat **10g**; Saturated Fat **2g**

Want to get the most flavor out of your fruit? Just add heat! The process of roasting pushes fruits' innate sugars up to the surface where they caramelize, intensifying their natural sweetness. Using roasted peaches in place of raw adds another layer of flavor to this smoothie, eliminating the need to add sugar to a drink that still tastes indulgent. Roasted nectarines or pineapple are both great substitutes. I love the hit of citrus that the zest adds, but feel free to leave it out if you don't have an orange hanging around the house.

1. Preheat the oven to 375°F.

2. Combine the peaches and cinnamon on a rimmed baking sheet and roast, turning once, until the peaches are very soft and caramelized, about 25 minutes. Remove to a plate and let cool completely. The fruit can be roasted up to 2 days ahead of time and stored in the refrigerator in a container with a tight-fitting lid.

3. In a blender, combine the fruit, yogurt, pistachios, orange zest, if using, vanilla, and a splash of water, and blend until smooth. Add the ice and blend again until smooth. Divide between 2 large glasses.

Easy Being Green Smoothie

SERVES 2

2 cups (packed) chopped Swiss chard or baby spinach

2 kiwis, peeled and chopped

1 cup seedless green grapes, frozen

1 cup frozen sliced peaches or mangoes

1 small Granny Smith apple, seeded and chopped

1 cup frozen pineapple chunks

Juice of 1 lime

1 cup ice cubes

PER SERVING: Calories **260**; Protein **3g**; Carbohydrates **60g**; Dietary Fiber **8g**; Sugar **47g**; Total Fat **1g**; Saturated Fat **0g**

This is a tasty green smoothie you'll actually want to drink, not one of those that is hard to choke down because it has greens and not much else. Fruit—including kiwi, grapes, peaches, apple, and pineapple—add a welcome touch of sweetness and body to this verdant smoothie. Kiwi doesn't get the respect that it deserves and typically only shows up in those French fruit tarts or as a garnish on pre-cut fruit salad, but those furry brown skins hide a really tasty, super-nutritional treat! Its flavor is a cross between that of a banana and a strawberry (yum), and, as it happens, the kiwi packs more vitamin C than an orange and is loaded with fiber and other valuable nutrients. Nutritious Swiss chard or baby spinach amp up the green factor and add a dose of iron.

In a blender, combine the greens, kiwis, grapes, peaches, apple, pineapple, lime juice, and ice cubes and blend until smooth. Divide between 2 large glasses.

Coffee Hazelnut Smoothie

SERVES 2

2 cups brewed strong coffee or
    espresso, cooled

1 cup skim, almond, or soy milk

½ cup 2% Greek yogurt

1 tablespoon chocolate hazelnut
    spread

1 small ripe banana, cut into pieces,
    frozen

1 tablespoon ground flaxseeds
    (optional)

PER SERVING: Calories **164**;
Protein **5g**; Carbohydrates **22g**;
Dietary Fiber **2g**; Sugar **19g**;
Total Fat **6g**; Saturated Fat **2g**

I love starting my day off with a cup of coffee . . . or ten. But I know that too much caffeine is not a good thing and when it comes to nutritional value, a cup of coffee has absolutely none. Here is a way to get my caffeine fix as well as some essential protein, carbs, and fiber. I always have coffee ice cubes on hand to throw into a smoothie or an iced coffee. Just save up the leftovers from your coffee pot each day and, once cool, pour into an ice cube tray and freeze. Pop the solid cubes into a freezer bag and your iced coffee–coffee smoothie future is bright!

Flaxseeds might be tiny, but a load of nutrition is packed into these little gems. For about 40 calories and 3 grams of fat, a tablespoon of ground flaxseeds will add essential vitamins and minerals—and a mild nutty flavor—to your favorite smoothie.

1. Pour the coffee into ice cube trays and freeze until firm, about 2 hours.

2. In a blender, combine the milk, yogurt, chocolate hazelnut spread, banana, flaxseeds, if using, and coffee ice cubes and blend until smooth. Divide between 2 large glasses and serve.

VARIATION

Coffee Chunky Monkey Smoothie

Substitute natural peanut butter for the chocolate hazelnut spread and add 2 teaspoons best-quality unsweetened cocoa powder, such as Ghirardelli. Calories **176**; Protein **7g**; Carbohydrates **20g**; Dietary Fiber **3g**; Sugar **14g**; Total Fat **8g**

Blueberry-Pomegranate Smoothie Soup with Quinoa Croutons

SERVES 4

1 cup old-fashioned rolled oats, such as Bob's Red Mill

¾ cup pomegranate juice

2 tablespoons pomegranate molasses

1 banana, halved, frozen

2 cups frozen organic wild blueberries, plus a few extra for garnish

½ cup 2% Greek yogurt, plus 2 tablespoons for garnish

Juice of ½ lemon

2 teaspoons freshly grated orange zest

2 teaspoons honey

2 tablespoons pomegranate seeds, for garnish (optional)

12 Quinoa Croutons (page 40)

PER SERVING: Calories **467**; Protein **12g**; Carbohydrates **72g**; Dietary Fiber **9g**; Sugar **30g**; Total Fat **15g**; Saturated Fat **7g**

Whether you drink it or use a spoon to eat it, this smoothie soup is nutritious and outrageously delicious. Yummy "croutons" made from quinoa and oats add terrific crunch and an additional dose of protein to the yogurt—helping this hold you until lunchtime. Make this just before you go to bed, and breakfast is ready to go when you are in the morning.

1. Put the oats in a blender and blend until they become powder-like. Add the pomegranate juice, pomegranate molasses, banana, blueberries, ½ cup yogurt, and the lemon juice and blend until smooth. Add the orange zest and honey and blend for a few more seconds.

2. Transfer the mixture to a container with a tight-fitting lid and refrigerate for at least 8 hours and up to 24 hours (this will help create a smoother consistency as the oats will absorb some of the liquid and become thicker).

3. Divide between 2 bowls, topping each with a tablespoon of yogurt, a few berries, pomegranate seeds, if using, and 6 quinoa croutons.

Persian Baked Omelet with Fresh Herbs

SERVES 6 TO 8

2 tablespoons olive oil

1 tablespoon unsalted butter

1 large red onion, halved and thinly sliced

Nonstick cooking spray

4 green onions, white and pale green parts, finely chopped

2 garlic cloves, finely chopped

2 ounces baby spinach, coarsely chopped

¼ cup fresh cilantro, finely chopped

¼ cup fresh flat-leaf parsley, finely chopped

¼ cup finely chopped fresh chives

2 tablespoons finely chopped fresh dill

¼ cup pine nuts, lightly toasted and chopped

Kosher salt and freshly ground black pepper

9 large eggs

¼ cup skim milk

½ cup 2% Greek yogurt

PER SERVING: Calories **238**; Protein **13g**; Carbohydrates **8g**; Dietary Fiber **2g**; Sugar **4g**; Total Fat **17g**; Saturated Fat **5g**

Persian cuisine is often simple and healthy, and is always flavorful. This omelet, with its heady base of red and green onions and garlic and loads of fresh herbs for bright flavor, is a perfect example.

1. In a large nonstick sauté pan, heat the oil and butter over medium heat until the oil begins to shimmer. Add the red onion and cook, stirring occasionally, until softened and caramelized, about 30 minutes.

2. Preheat the oven to 350°F. Spray a 9-inch ovenproof nonstick pan with nonstick spray.

3. Add the green onions and garlic to the caramelized onion and cook for 2 minutes. Stir in the spinach and cook until the leaves begin to wilt, 2 minutes. Add the cilantro, parsley, chives, dill, and pine nuts, season with salt and pepper, and remove from the heat. Transfer to the prepared pan and put in the oven for 5 minutes.

4. Meanwhile, in a blender, blend the eggs and milk on low for about 30 seconds. Pour the eggs over the veggie mixture in the pan, return to the oven, and bake until puffed, just set, and lightly golden brown on top, about 20 minutes.

5. Remove the omelet and let cool for 5 minutes on a baking rack. Transfer to a platter, slice into wedges, and top with the yogurt.

Baked Egg Muffins with Piperade and Garlic Bread Crumbs

This is my kind of egg muffin; forget the rubbery, bland drive-thru variety. Piperade is a full-flavored pepper relish from the Basque region of Spain often served with eggs. Adding mixed greens and just a sprinkling of bread crumbs keeps this dish low on carbs and calories, making it a really healthy breakfast or even a light lunch.

SERVES 4

Piperade

Nonstick cooking spray

2 tablespoons olive oil

1 small Spanish onion, halved and thinly sliced

1 small red bell pepper, halved, seeded, and thinly sliced crosswise

1 small poblano chile, halved and thinly sliced crosswise

1 garlic clove, finely chopped

1 teaspoon smoked paprika

4 plum tomatoes, seeded and diced

Kosher salt and freshly ground black pepper

2 tablespoons chopped fresh flat-leaf parsley

8 large eggs

Mixed Greens

4 ounces mixed baby greens

1 tablespoon red wine vinegar

1 tablespoon extra-virgin olive oil

Kosher salt and freshly ground black pepper

Garlic Bread Crumbs (recipe follows)

PER SERVING (INCLUDES BREAD CRUMBS): Calories **390**; Protein **16g**; Carbohydrates **18g**; Dietary Fiber **3g**; Sugar **6g**; Total Fat **28g**; Saturated Fat **6g**

1. Make the piperade: Preheat the oven to 375°F. Lightly spray 8 muffin cups out of a 12-cup muffin tin with nonstick spray.

2. Heat the oil in a large sauté pan over medium-high heat until it begins to shimmer. Add the onion, bell pepper, and poblano and cook, stirring occasionally, until soft, about 6 minutes. Add the garlic and cook for 30 seconds. Stir in the paprika and cook for 30 seconds. Add the tomatoes and ½ cup water, season with salt and black pepper, and simmer until the tomatoes are soft and the mixture is thick, about 20 minutes. Stir in the parsley.

3. Divide the piperade among the 8 prepared muffin cups and, using the back of a spoon, press gently to make the tops even. Crack an egg into each cup and season with salt and black pepper. Bake until the whites are set and the yolks are still runny, about 8 minutes.

4. Season the greens: Put the greens in a bowl, add the vinegar and oil, season with salt and black pepper, and toss to coat.

5. Divide the greens among 4 plates. Remove the eggs from the oven, sprinkle the tops with the bread crumbs, and using an offset spatula, carefully remove from the tin. Serve the eggs on top of the greens.

Garlic Bread Crumbs

MAKES ½ CUP

2 tablespoons olive oil

2 garlic cloves, smashed

Kosher salt and freshly ground black pepper

2 slices good-quality white or wheat bread, crust removed, processed into fine bread crumbs

1. In a small sauté pan, heat the oil over medium heat until it shimmers. Add the garlic and salt and pepper and cook until the garlic is light golden brown. Remove from the heat and let the garlic infuse the oil for 5 minutes.

2. Discard the garlic and then return the pan to the stove over medium heat. Add the bread crumbs and cook in the oil, stirring constantly, until golden brown and crisp, about 5 minutes. Serve immediately or let cool, cover, and store for up to 2 days at room temperature.

PER TABLESPOON: Calories **55**; Protein **1g**; Carbohydrates **5g**; Dietary Fiber **1g**; Sugar **1g**; Total Fat **4g**; Saturated Fat **0g**

Avocado Toast with Red Chile and Cilantro

SERVES 2

1 ripe Hass avocado, peeled and pitted

½ fresno pepper, finely diced

Juice of 1 lime

2 tablespoons chopped fresh cilantro

2 slices whole-grain toast (such as 12-grain, whole wheat, or oat bran), brushed with extra-virgin olive oil

Coarse sea salt

PER SERVING: Calories **225**; Protein **5g**; Carbohydrates **23g**; Dietary Fiber **8g**; Sugar **2g**; Total Fat **13g**; Saturated Fat **2g**

Avocado toast has hit such a fever pitch (thank you, Instagram!) that some people are saying they're over it. Not me. Packed with fiber and heart-healthy monounsaturated fatty acids, avocados contain more potassium than a banana. And their creamy texture and rich flavor are simply made for a crunchy slice of toast; this is a near-perfect combination.

Put the avocado in a bowl and coarsely mash with a fork. Stir in the fresno pepper, lime juice, and cilantro. Divide between the slices of toast and sprinkle with sea salt.

Israeli Breakfast Sandwich

SERVES 4

Roasted Eggplant

1 small eggplant, cut crosswise into ½-inch slices

2 tablespoons olive oil

Kosher salt and freshly ground black pepper

Israeli Salad

1 small English cucumber, cut into ½-inch dice

2 plum tomatoes, seeded and cut into ½-inch dice

Juice of 1 lemon

1 tablespoon red wine vinegar

2 tablespoons extra-virgin olive oil

3 tablespoons finely chopped fresh flat-leaf parsley

Kosher salt and freshly ground black pepper

4 whole-wheat pita

1 cup hummus, homemade (pages 102–105) or store-bought

1 cup finely shredded red cabbage

Amba or mango hot sauce

4 large eggs, hard-cooked and thinly sliced

PER SERVING: Calories **440**; Protein **16g**; Carbohydrates **36g**; Dietary Fiber **9g**; Sugar **7g**; Total Fat **26g**; Saturated Fat **5g**

This delicious and incredibly healthy sandwich is called sabich in Israel. If you don't feel like making all of the components from scratch, feel free to purchase prepared hummus and even Israeli salad from your local deli, salad bar, or grocery store. This is typically served with a mango-based sauce called amba. I think that a good-quality mango hot sauce works just as well so that's what I call for in this recipe to make things a bit simpler.

1. Roast the eggplant: Preheat the oven to 400°F.

2. Brush the eggplant slices with the oil on both sides and season with salt and pepper. Put in a single layer on a rimmed baking sheet and roast until golden brown and soft, about 30 minutes.

3. Make the Israeli salad: In a medium bowl, combine the cucumber, tomatoes, lemon juice, vinegar, extra-virgin olive oil, and parsley and season with salt and pepper. Let sit at room temperature for at least 30 minutes. (You can also make this a day in advance and store, covered, in the refrigerator.)

4. Toast the pita: Wrap the pita tightly in foil and let it warm in the oven for 5 minutes.

5. To serve: Slice 1 inch from the top of each pita and open the pocket. Spread ¼ cup of the hummus on one side of each pocket, then add some eggplant, a few spoonfuls of the Israeli salad, some cabbage, and a few dashes of the sauce. Stuff each pita with a sliced egg.

Savory Yogurt Bowl with Chickpeas, Cucumber, and Beets

SERVES 2

1 tablespoon tahini paste

3 tablespoons fresh lemon juice

⅛ teaspoon chile powder

⅛ teaspoon ground turmeric

Kosher salt and freshly ground black pepper

½ cup canned chickpeas, drained, rinsed, and drained again

1 cup diced Persian cucumber

1 tablespoon red wine vinegar

1 tablespoon chopped fresh dill

1 small beet, peeled and grated

⅛ teaspoon ground cumin

1 tablespoon chopped fresh flat-leaf parsley

1 cup 2% Greek yogurt

1 tablespoon extra-virgin olive oil

1 tablespoon chopped toasted pistachios

1 tablespoon toasted fennel seeds (see page 28)

PER SERVING: Calories **337**; Protein **16g**; Carbohydrates **32g**; Dietary Fiber **7g**; Sugar **12g**; Total Fat **16g**; Saturated Fat **4g**

Yogurt for breakfast doesn't always have to be paired with fruit, granola, and honey. This savory yogurt bowl contains some of my favorite ingredients, but you can mix and match all day. Try trading chickpeas for black beans or edamame, and experiment with different vegetables such as asparagus, kale, or spinach. Pistachios work particularly well with the Middle Eastern–inspired flavors here, but feel free to add any nut you like.

1. In a small bowl, whisk together the tahini, 2 tablespoons of the lemon juice, the chile powder, turmeric, and salt and pepper to taste. Add the chickpeas and toss to coat.

2. In a second bowl, toss together the cucumber, red wine vinegar, dill, and salt and pepper to taste.

3. In a third bowl, combine the beet, cumin, parsley, and the remaining 1 tablespoon lemon juice, season with salt and pepper, and toss to combine.

4. Scoop the yogurt into a serving bowl. Spoon the chickpeas, cucumber, and beet into the bowl. Drizzle the olive oil over everything. Garnish with the pistachios and fennel seeds.

Homemade Toasted Muesli Three Ways

The first place I remember seeing muesli is at the breakfast buffet table while once on vacation in Europe. This mixture of nuts, grains, and dried fruit has been touted as a healthy breakfast staple in Switzerland and Germany for centuries. Unlike its cousin, granola, which is usually laced with sugar and baked with some form of fat, muesli has no added oil, and it is very rarely, if ever, sweetened. In a break from tradition, I toast the nuts and grains lightly to impart a richer, deeper flavor. This recipe includes my favorite grains, nuts, and dried fruits, but feel free to experiment with your own favorites.

Toasted Muesli

MAKES ABOUT 6 CUPS

1½ cups old-fashioned rolled oats

1 cup barley flakes

1 cup rye flakes

½ cup flaxseed meal

½ cup shelled pumpkin seeds

½ cup chopped almonds

¼ cup hazelnuts or pistachios, chopped

¼ cup golden raisins

¼ cup dried cherries or cranberries

¼ cup chopped dried apricots or dates

Pinch of sea salt

PER ½ CUP: Calories **265**; Protein **10g**; Carbohydrates **32g**; Dietary Fiber **6g**; Sugar **6g**; Total Fat **11g**; Saturated Fat **1g**

1. Preheat the oven to 325°F.

2. Spread the oats, barley flakes, rye flakes, flaxseed meal, pumpkin seeds, almonds, and hazelnuts on a large rimmed baking sheet and bake, stirring once, until lightly golden brown, about 10 minutes. Remove from the oven and let cool.

3. Add the dried fruit and salt to the mixture on the baking sheet and stir to combine. Transfer to a container with a lid and store in a cool, dry place. The muesli will last for at least a month if stored properly.

Overnight Muesli with Banana Yogurt Cream

SERVES 2

2 large super-ripe bananas, peeled and frozen

½ cup pourable plain yogurt (such as Ronnybrook)

¼ teaspoon ground cinnamon

1 cup Toasted Muesli (page 67), plus 2 tablespoons for serving

PER SERVING: Calories **479**; Protein **15g**; Carbohydrates **71g**; Dietary Fiber **11g**; Sugar **35g**; Total Fat **15g**; Saturated Fat **3g**

Frozen ripe bananas—the darker skinned, the better—become a thick, dessert-worthy but breakfast-appropriate cream when mixed with pourable yogurt. Add muesli to the mix and you've got an outrageously good take on overnight refrigerator oats. Drizzle this with honey, pure maple syrup, or agave syrup if you want an extra hit of sweetness.

1. In a blender, combine the bananas, yogurt, cinnamon, and a splash of water, and blend until very smooth and creamy, about 2 minutes.

2. Divide the yogurt mixture between 2 bowls, add ½ cup of the muesli to each, and stir to combine. Cover and refrigerate overnight.

3. In the morning, top each with a tablespoon of muesli.

Warm Apple Muesli Porridge

SERVES 2

1 cup apple cider

1 cinnamon stick

2 whole cloves

2-inch piece of orange zest

1 small Granny Smith apple, halved and coarsely grated

1 small Gala apple, halved and coarsely grated

2 cups skim, almond, or soy milk or water

1 cup Toasted Muesli (page 67)

PER SERVING: Calories **480**; Protein **19g**; Carbohydrates **77g**; Dietary Fiber **9g**; Sugar **45g**; Total Fat **11g**; Saturated Fat **1g**

Grated apple and milk are classic ingredients in Bircher muesli—a traditional preparation of muesli mixed with fruit and juice, milk, or water and yogurt and soaked overnight—and were a starting point for this recipe. The other inspiration was on the opposite side of the spectrum: those way-too-sweet, just barely apple-y packets of apple-cinnamon oatmeal I used to eat as a kid. This porridge takes the best of each, making for one warm, comforting, healthy, and delicious breakfast.

1. In a medium saucepan, combine the apple cider, cinnamon stick, cloves, and orange zest, bring to a boil over high heat, and cook until reduced to ¼ cup. Add the apples and cook until soft, about 5 minutes. Add the milk and bring to a simmer. Remove from the heat, cover, and let steep for 5 minutes. Discard the cinnamon stick, cloves, and orange zest.

2. Return the mixture to a simmer, add 1 cup of the muesli, and cook for 1 minute. Spoon into bowls and serve.

Muesli Bites with Toasted Coconut

MAKES 16 BITES

¾ cup sweetened shredded coconut

½ cup natural nut or seed butter

1 tablespoon honey, agave syrup, or pure maple syrup

Pinch of fine sea salt

1 cup Toasted Muesli (page 67)

PER BITE: Calories **217**; Protein **7g**; Carbohydrates **12g**; Dietary Fiber **4g**; Sugar **5g**; Total Fat **16g**; Saturated Fat **3g**

Add some almond butter (or the nut or seed butter of your choice) to muesli, roll into a ball, and toss in another layer of nutty crunch, and you not only have something as delicious as it is nutritious but also a portable treat at that! Perfect as a pre- or post-workout bite, these also make a sweet lunch-box treat or after-school snack that you can feel very good about serving.

1. Preheat the oven to 325°F. Line a rimmed baking sheet with parchment paper.

2. Spread the coconut on the baking sheet in an even layer and toast in the oven, stirring several times, until lightly golden brown and crisp, about 10 minutes. Remove and let cool completely (it will get crisper as it sits).

3. Put the toasted coconut in a zip-top plastic bag and crush with a rolling pin, or process briefly in a food processor or blender. Spread on a large plate. Reserve the parchment-lined baking sheet.

4. In a small saucepan, whisk together the nut butter, honey, and salt and heat over low heat until melted; or combine in a bowl and microwave for 30 seconds, stirring once after 15 seconds.

5. Add the muesli to the nut butter mixture and mix to combine. Using a ½-ounce (or 1-tablespoon) ice cream scoop or small spoons, make small balls and then roll each in the coconut. Transfer to the prepared baking sheet and refrigerate until firm, about 15 minutes. Store in a single layer in a covered container in the refrigerator.

PB&J Cream of Wheat

SERVES 4

Nonstick cooking spray

2 cups black seedless grapes

2 tablespoons peanut butter

1 cup skim milk

⅛ teaspoon fine sea salt

½ cup creamy wheat cereal, such as Bob's Red Mill

¼ cup roasted peanuts, chopped

PER SERVING: Calories **262**; Protein **9g**; Carbohydrates **37g**; Dietary Fiber **3g**; Sugar **17g**; Total Fat **9g**; Saturated Fat **1g**

I feel like when I was growing up, there were two kinds of households: those that ate oatmeal and those that ate farina (also known by one of its commercial names, Cream of Wheat). Ours was an oatmeal house, but I had friends who lived in farina houses and childhood sleepovers brought about my first tastes of that other breakfast porridge. My inspiration for this bowl of morning goodness actually comes from yet another childhood favorite: whole-wheat toast with peanut butter and jelly. My jelly of choice was grape back then, and so grapes are the fruit I go for here, but you can certainly roast strawberries or raspberries instead. The same goes for the peanut butter; try this with almond or cashew butter as an alternative.

1. Preheat the oven to 375°F.

2. Lightly spray an 8-inch baking dish with nonstick spray, add the grapes and 2 tablespoons water, and cover the dish with aluminum foil. Roast, stirring once, until soft, about 25 minutes. Remove the foil and continue roasting until slightly caramelized, about 10 minutes longer.

3. Put the peanut butter in a heat-proof ramekin and heat briefly in a microwave (or in the oven) to melt slightly.

4. In a medium saucepan, combine the milk, 1½ cups water, and the salt and bring to a boil over high heat. Slowly whisk in the wheat cereal, stirring constantly. Lower the heat and simmer until smooth and thickened, about 4 minutes, adding more water to keep it creamy.

5. To serve, spoon into bowls and top with a drizzle of peanut butter and the roasted grapes. Sprinkle with the nuts.

VARIATION

Maple-Cashew Cream of Wheat

Replace the peanut butter with cashew butter and add 2 tablespoons pure maple syrup. Garnish with chopped roasted cashews. Calories **294**; Carbohydrates **45g**; Dietary Fiber **2g**; Sugar **24g**; Saturated Fat **2g**

Oatmeal with Ricotta,
Chocolate, Orange,
and Pistachio

Overnight Oatmeal
Three Ways

Using this method to cook steel-cut oatmeal is a serious
no-brainer: a mere two minutes of prep the night before cuts
thirty minutes off of your cooking time *and* produces really
creamy oats. Good oatmeal does more than comfort your soul;
it fuels your body. Fiber-rich and full of calcium and potassium,
oatmeal is a blank canvas for a spectrum of dried and fresh
fruits, nuts, nut butters, seeds, and even savory toppings like
a perfectly poached egg and crisp shards of bacon.

Oatmeal with Apricot,
Tahini, and Sesame

Savory Oatmeal with Poached
Egg, Parmesan, and Bacon

Overnight Oatmeal

MAKES 4 CUPS; SERVES 4

Pinch of fine sea salt

1 cup steel-cut oats

PER SERVING: Calories **152**; Protein **5g**; Carbohydrates **27g**; Dietary Fiber **4g**; Sugar **1g**; Total Fat **3g**; Saturated Fat **0g**

1. In a medium saucepan, bring 4 cups water to a boil, stir in the salt and oats, and cook for 1 minute. Remove from the heat, cover the pan, and let cool to room temperature. Transfer the pan to the refrigerator and let sit for at least 5 hours and up to 12 hours.

2. Remove the lid, set the pan over medium heat, and cook until the liquid is absorbed and the oatmeal has thickened and is heated through, about 10 minutes, adding a splash more water if needed. Eat plain or see the following toppings. Leftover cooked oatmeal will last for up to 1 week, tightly covered in the refrigerator. Reheat in the microwave or on the stovetop, adding a little extra water if needed.

Savory Oatmeal with Poached Egg, Parmesan, and Bacon

SERVES 1

2 teaspoons white vinegar

1 large egg

Kosher salt

1 cup Overnight Oatmeal (above), hot

⅛ teaspoon coarsely ground black pepper

A few thin shavings of Parmigiano-Reggiano cheese

1 slice bacon, cooked until crisp, crumbled

Chopped fresh flat-leaf parsley (optional)

PER SERVING: Calories **255**; Protein **14g**; Carbohydrates **28g**; Dietary Fiber **4g**; Sugar **1g**; Total Fat **10g**; Saturated Fat **3g**

Don't laugh or roll your eyes—I swear this combo makes total sense. I was skeptical at first, too, and then it hit me: this is like a bowl of American polenta! With that in mind, I thought about some of my other Italian favorites, and spaghetti carbonara gets special billing on that list. I could eat a pound of it myself, but all that pasta, eggs, cheese, and guanciale—I would have to run an entire New York marathon just to work off the calories! This dish gives me all of those savory, satisfying flavors but in a much healthier package. It's a substantial way to start your day and also makes a great lunch.

1. In a medium, high-sided pan, bring 4 cups water to a simmer over medium heat. Add the vinegar. Crack an egg into a ramekin and season with salt. Slide the egg into the water and cook until the white is just set but the yolk is still runny, about 4 minutes. Remove with a slotted spoon to a plate lined with a paper towel to drain.

2. Put the warm oatmeal in a bowl and top with the egg, pepper, cheese, bacon, and parsley, if desired.

Oatmeal with Ricotta, Chocolate, Orange, and Pistachio

SERVES 1

1 cup Overnight Oatmeal (page 73), hot

1 tablespoon orange marmalade

2 tablespoons part-skim ricotta

1 tablespoon chopped toasted pistachios

1 tablespoon grated bittersweet chocolate

PER SERVING: Calories **358**; Protein **12g**; Carbohydrates **47g**; Dietary Fiber **6g**; Sugar **15g**; Total Fat **14g**; Saturated Fat **5g**

When you crave something decadent and chocolaty but still want to keep your breakfast in check, this oatmeal should do the trick. It's kind of like a healthy cannoli bowl! I love creamy ricotta, and the part-skim variety is an excellent low-fat dairy source. Bittersweet chocolate is the healthiest of all chocolate—just be sure that you get a high-quality variety with at least 70 percent cacao.

Spoon the hot oatmeal into a bowl, top with the marmalade and ricotta, and garnish with the pistachios and chocolate.

Oatmeal with Apricot, Tahini, and Sesame

SERVES 1

3 dried apricots

1 cup Overnight Oatmeal (page 73), hot

1 teaspoon light brown sugar

1 teaspoon tahini

1 teaspoon toasted sesame seeds

PER SERVING: Calories **245**; Protein **7g**; Carbohydrates **39g**; Dietary Fiber **5g**; Sugar **9g**; Total Fat **7g**; Saturated Fat **1g**

I like to think of this combination of toppings as a Middle Eastern PB&J! Tahini is a rich, thick paste made from sesame seeds; one little tablespoon adds loads of rich flavor and creaminess to a bowl of oatmeal. The toasted seeds punch up that nutty flavor and are a nice textural addition as well. Dried apricots, one of my favorite dried fruits, are a perfect sweet foil to the nutty sesame flavors in play, and they also provide a boost of iron, magnesium, and vitamin A.

1. Soak the apricots in warm water for 10 minutes to soften. Drain and slice them.

2. Put the hot oatmeal in a bowl and stir in the brown sugar until dissolved. Top with the apricots, drizzle with the tahini, and sprinkle the sesame seeds on top.

Whole-Wheat Muesli Pancakes with Maple Pear Butter

SERVES 4

A combination of whole-wheat flour and fruit-and-nut-laden muesli makes these delicious pancakes a virtuous way to start your day. Pear butter is so rich and creamy that it tastes much more decadent than it really is—there's some maple syrup to help sweeten the deal, but ripe pears are a naturally sweet starting point. Cinnamon, nutmeg, ginger, and cloves add autumnal flavor.

1 cup low-fat buttermilk

¾ cup muesli, homemade (page 67) or store-bought

¾ cup whole-wheat flour

2 teaspoons baking powder

¼ teaspoon fine sea salt

1 large egg

2 tablespoons light brown sugar

2 tablespoons canola oil

1 teaspoon pure vanilla extract

Nonstick cooking spray

½ cup Maple Pear Butter (recipe follows)

PER SERVING (INCLUDES PEAR BUTTER): Calories **383**; Protein **11g**; Carbohydrates **54g**; Dietary Fiber **6g**; Sugar **25g**; Total Fat **14g**; Saturated Fat **2g**

1. In a medium bowl, mix together the buttermilk and muesli; let stand for 15 minutes.

2. In a small bowl, whisk together the flour, baking powder, and salt. In another small bowl, whisk together the egg, brown sugar, oil, and vanilla until smooth. Stir the egg mixture into the muesli mixture and then fold in the flour mixture until just combined. Do not overmix. Let rest for 15 minutes.

3. Heat a griddle to 350°F or a large nonstick sauté pan over medium-high heat and spray with nonstick spray.

4. For each pancake, scoop a little less than ¼ cup batter onto the hot griddle and cook until the bottom is golden brown and small bubbles appear on the surface, about 3 minutes. Flip over and continue cooking until the bottom is golden brown, about 2 minutes longer.

5. Serve 3 pancakes per order topped with pear butter.

Maple Pear Butter

MAKES ABOUT 1½ CUPS

2 pounds ripe pears, peeled, cored, and diced

¼ cup plus 2 tablespoons pure maple syrup

1 tablespoon fresh lemon juice

1 teaspoon ground cinnamon

½ teaspoon ground ginger

⅛ teaspoon ground nutmeg

⅛ teaspoon ground cloves

1. In a medium saucepan, stir all ingredients together and bring to a boil over medium-high heat. Reduce the heat to medium-low and simmer, partially covering with a lid and stirring occasionally, until thickened, about 50 minutes. Keep an eye on the mixture so that the bottom does not burn.

2. Remove from the heat and, if you want a smooth pear butter, transfer to a food processor. Pulse until smooth. Skip this step if you prefer your pear butter chunky.

3. Transfer to a jar with a lid and let cool. Cover and refrigerate for up to a week.

PER TABLESPOON: Calories **36**; Protein **0g**; Carbohydrates **9g**; Dietary Fiber **1g**; Sugar **7g**; Total Fat **0g**; Saturated Fat **0g**

Spelt Waffles with Blueberry Compote and Lemon Ricotta Cream

SERVES 6

Lemon Ricotta Cream

1 cup part-skim ricotta

1 tablespoon confectioners' sugar

1 teaspoon grated lemon zest, plus more for garnish

1 teaspoon fresh lemon juice

Blueberry Compote

1 pint fresh blueberries, or 1 pound frozen blueberries, thawed

2 tablespoons honey or pure maple syrup

1 teaspoon fresh lemon juice

Waffles

1 cup spelt flour

1 cup whole-wheat flour

1 tablespoon granulated sugar

2 teaspoons baking powder

1 teaspoon baking soda

⅛ teaspoon fine sea salt

2 cups low-fat buttermilk

5 tablespoons unsalted butter, melted

2 large eggs

1 teaspoon finely grated lemon zest

Nonstick cooking spray

PER SERVING: Calories **411**; Protein **15g**; Carbohydrates **53g**; Dietary Fiber **7g**; Sugar **19g**; Total Fat **16g**; Saturated Fat **9g**

Making waffles with ingredients such as whole-wheat and spelt flour can be tricky; there is a fine line between light and fluffy and leaden and flat. It took some research, but I think I figured out the perfect ratio of ingredients to produce one really amazing waffle: delicious *and* healthy. Blueberries make every breakfast better, plus they are full of antioxidants. Finally, while there's nothing fake about it, this whipped cream fake-out of part-skim ricotta will fool your taste buds, for sure.

1. Make the ricotta cream: In a small bowl, combine the ricotta, confectioners' sugar, lemon zest, and lemon juice and whisk until light and fluffy. Cover and refrigerate for at least 30 minutes and up to 2 hours to allow the flavors to meld.

2. Make the compote: In a small saucepan, combine the blueberries, ¼ cup water, and the honey and bring to a simmer over medium heat. Cook until the mixture thickens, about 7 minutes. Transfer to a bowl, add the lemon juice, and let cool at least slightly.

3. Make the waffles: Preheat the oven to 275°F; set a rack on a baking sheet and put in the oven.

4. In a medium bowl, whisk together the flours, granulated sugar, baking powder, baking soda, and salt. In a large bowl, whisk together the buttermilk, butter, eggs, and lemon zest. Add the flour mixture, and mix just until the batter is combined. Let rest for 15 minutes.

5. Heat a waffle iron according to the manufacturer's instructions; spray with nonstick spray. Pour batter onto the iron (the amount depends on the size of the iron), leaving a ½-inch border on all sides. Close the iron and cook until the waffle is golden brown and crisp, 3 to 5 minutes. Transfer to the rack in the oven to keep warm; repeat with the remaining batter.

6. To serve, top the waffles with the blueberry compote and ricotta cream. Garnish with lemon zest.

Mini Zucchini-Banana Muffins with Berry Chia Jam

MAKES 24 MINI OR 12 REGULAR-SIZE MUFFINS

Nonstick cooking spray

1 cup unbleached all-purpose flour

¾ cup whole-wheat flour

½ cup ground flaxseeds

2 teaspoons baking soda

1 teaspoon baking powder

½ teaspoon coarse salt

1 teaspoon ground cinnamon

Pinch of ground nutmeg

1 large egg

¼ cup lightly packed light-brown sugar

¼ cup granulated sugar

¾ cup low-fat buttermilk

1 teaspoon pure vanilla extract

1½ cups coarsely grated zucchini (from 1 large zucchini), squeezed in a clean dish towel or paper towels

⅓ cup mashed banana (from 1 large overly ripe banana)

Berry Chia Jam (recipe follows)

PER SERVING (2 MINI MUFFINS OR 1 MUFFIN; INCLUDES JAM): Calories **148**; Protein **5g**; Carbohydrates **26g**; Dietary Fiber **3g**; Sugar **11g**; Total Fat **3g**; Saturated Fat **1g**

These muffins are moist but have no oil or butter in them. Their secret? A banana stirred into the batter. Add grated zucchini and you have even more moisture and beneficial fiber in the mix. The chia jam is an easy way to make your own fresh fruit spread in minutes, no cooking required. The fiber in chia seeds (those nutritional wonders) expands in water, becoming a gel-like substance that thickens mashed berries without altering their fresh flavor.

1. Preheat the oven to 350°F. Lightly coat 24 mini muffin cups or 12 standard muffin cups with nonstick spray.

2. In a large bowl, whisk together the flours, flaxseeds, baking soda, baking powder, salt, cinnamon, and nutmeg.

3. In a medium bowl, whisk the egg until smooth. Whisk in the sugars and then the buttermilk and vanilla and mix. Stir in the zucchini and banana. Add the milk mixture to the flour mixture and mix until just combined. Do not overmix or the muffins will be tough.

4. Fill the prepared muffin cups three-quarters of the way with the mixture. Bake until a skewer inserted into the center has a few moist crumbs attached, 10 minutes. Let cool in the pan on a baking racking for 5 minutes, then remove and let cool for an additional 5 minutes. Serve with the berry chia jam.

Berry Chia Jam

MAKES 1 CUP

¼ cup chia seeds (black or white)

2 cups fresh berries or frozen, thawed (strawberries, raspberries, blackberries, or a combination)

1 tablespoon all-natural fruit jam

2 tablespoons fresh lemon juice

1. In a small bowl, combine the chia seeds and ½ cup water and set aside for 10 minutes.

2. In a medium bowl, combine the berries, jam, and lemon juice and mash to a jam-like consistency with a fork.

3. Spoon the hydrated chia seeds into the berry mixture and stir to combine, using the fork to break up lumps of chia. Cover and refrigerate for 30 minutes to allow the jam to thicken more. The jam will keep for up to a week, covered and refrigerated.

PER TABLESPOON: Calories **25**; Protein **1g**; Carbohydrates **4g**; Dietary Fiber **2g**; Sugar **2g**; Total Fat **1g**; Saturated Fat **0g**

Oatmeal Breakfast Cookies

MAKES 9 COOKIES

1 large overly ripe banana

½ cup crunchy almond butter

¼ cup pure maple syrup or honey

1 teaspoon pure vanilla extract

½ cup chopped dried apricots

¼ cup chopped dried cherries

⅛ teaspoon fine sea salt

2 cups old-fashioned rolled oats

2 tablespoons finely ground
  flaxseeds

1 teaspoon ground cinnamon

Nonstick cooking spray

PER COOKIE: Calories **259**;
Protein **7g**; Carbohydrates **36g**;
Dietary Fiber **5g**; Sugar **16g**;
Total Fat **10g**; Saturated Fat **2g**

These cookies are chock-full of good stuff: whole-grain oats, rich almond butter, dried fruits, cinnamon, and just a touch of maple syrup. I'd consider renaming these "Too Good to Be True" Breakfast Cookies if it weren't for the fact that they are loaded with fiber and protein—a great way to start any active day! If eating cookies (even healthy ones!) for breakfast isn't your thing, they're a great on-the-go snack to take on a hike or toss in a lunch box. You can also try them topped with yogurt and a drizzle of honey or, for a new spin on oatmeal, in a bowl with warm, frothy milk.

1. Put the banana in a medium bowl and mash using a potato masher or fork until smooth. Stir in the almond butter, maple syrup, and vanilla until smooth. Stir in the apricots, cherries, and salt. Let sit for 5 minutes. Mix in the oats, flaxseeds, and cinnamon until just combined. Cover and refrigerate for at least 30 minutes and up to 8 hours.

2. Preheat the oven to 350°F. Spray 9 cups of a 12-cup muffin tin with nonstick spray.

3. Divide the batter among the 9 muffin cups, smoothing the tops. Transfer to the oven and bake the cookies until golden brown and set, about 12 minutes. Cool in the pan on a baking rack for 10 minutes. Run an offset spatula or butter knife around the edge and gently remove and let cool completely on the baking rack, at least 30 minutes longer. The cookies will keep in a sealed container for up to 5 days.

ENERGY BOOSTERS AND SNACKS

Vanilla Bean and Espresso Granola

MAKES ABOUT 4 CUPS

2 tablespoons canola oil

1 tablespoon instant espresso powder

2 tablespoons hot coffee

2 tablespoons light brown sugar

Pinch of ground cinnamon

1 vanilla bean, split lengthwise, seeds scraped

1 teaspoon pure vanilla extract

1½ cups almonds, chopped

1½ cups old-fashioned rolled oats

¼ cup dark chocolate–covered espresso beans, coarsely chopped

PER ½ CUP: Calories **306**; Protein **9g**; Carbohydrates **21g**; Dietary Fiber **5g**; Sugar **5g**; Total Fat **21g**; Saturated Fat **3g**

Before I changed my ways, I used to stop by a popular coffee shop on my way to the office for a medium double-vanilla latte to start off my day. A few hours and one sugar crash later, I would follow it up with another. That is more than 500 empty calories and 12 grams of fat, all before noon! I love the flavor of coffee paired with anything, but I particular like it with vanilla and chocolate. Having sworn off the vanilla lattes, I now just do a skim-milk latte and eat a handful of this more nutritious latte-inspired granola instead. It is also great stirred into yogurt or sprinkled on oatmeal.

1. Preheat the oven to 325°F and line a rimmed baking sheet with parchment paper.

2. In a small bowl, whisk together the oil, espresso powder, coffee, brown sugar, cinnamon, vanilla bean seeds, and vanilla extract until combined. In another small bowl, mix together the almonds and oats. Add the almond mixture to the coffee mixture and toss to combine.

3. Transfer to the baking sheet in an even layer and bake for 15 minutes. Stir and then bake for another 10 minutes until lightly golden brown. Remove and let cool completely.

4. Break into small pieces, put in a bowl, and stir in the espresso beans.

Roasted Chickpeas

SERVES 6

2 tablespoons canola or olive oil

2 (15.5-ounce) cans chickpeas, drained, rinsed well, and drained well again on paper towels

Kosher salt and freshly ground black pepper

1 tablespoon any spice (curry powder, taco seasoning, chile powder) or spice blend (see pages 35–37), optional

1 teaspoon grated lemon or lime zest (optional)

PER SERVING: Calories **179**; Protein **7g**; Carbohydrates **23g**; Dietary Fiber **8g**; Sugar **0g**; Total Fat **7g**; Saturated Fat **0g**

You can find bags of these tasty, protein-laden crunchy legumes in many grocery and health food stores these days, but they are so incredibly easy to make, not to mention inexpensive, that you really should make them at home. As with all homemade snacks, the healthy advantage is that you can control the fat and salt that goes into them. Terrific eaten out of hand as a snack, roasted chickpeas are also excellent as a topping for soups, salads, or dips.

1. Preheat the oven to 400°F.

2. Heat the oil in a large ovenproof sauté pan over high heat until it begins to shimmer. Add the chickpeas and season with salt and pepper and spice, if using. Stir to make sure the chickpeas are evenly coated.

3. Transfer the chickpeas to the oven and roast, stirring once or twice, until the chickpeas are lightly golden brown and crisp, about 20 minutes.

4. Remove from the oven, add more salt, if desired, and stir in the zest, if using. Serve hot or at room temperature.

VARIATION

Cinnamon-Sugar Roasted Chickpeas

This one's for the person with a sweet tooth and can be a fun way to start your day instead of cinnamon toast. Omit the spice. Mix together 1 tablespoon sugar and 1 teaspoon ground cinnamon, add to the chickpeas just as they come out of the oven, and toss to coat. Calories **187**; Carbohydrates **25g**; Sugar **2g**

Raspberry–White Peach Granola Poppers

MAKES 36 POPPERS

3 cups old-fashioned rolled oats

¾ cup almonds, coarsely chopped

½ teaspoon ground cinnamon

⅛ teaspoon ground nutmeg

½ cup crushed freeze-dried raspberries

¼ cup honey, agave syrup, or pure maple syrup

¼ cup coconut oil

¼ cup almond butter

Pinch of fine sea salt

1 large egg white

1 teaspoon pure vanilla extract

¾ cup dried peaches, preferably white, chopped

PER POPPER: Calories **118**; Protein **3g**; Carbohydrates **11g**; Dietary Fiber **2g**; Sugar **4g**; Total Fat **7g**; Saturated Fat **2g**

Peaches and raspberries make one of my favorite fruit combinations. These tasty little bites are perfect for popping whenever you need a nutritious burst of energy.

1. Preheat the oven to 300°F. Line a rimmed baking sheet with parchment paper or a silicone baking mat.

2. In a large bowl, combine the oats, almonds, cinnamon, nutmeg, and crushed raspberries.

3. In a small saucepan, combine the honey, oil, almond butter, and salt and cook over low heat, whisking a few times, until melted. Remove from the heat and let cool for 5 minutes so the egg white doesn't scramble when added.

4. Whisk together the egg white and vanilla in a small bowl until fluffy and stir into the honey mixture. Pour over the oat mixture, add the peaches, and stir well to combine.

5. Using a #40 ice cream scoop (about 2 tablespoons), scoop balls of the granola and put them in an even layer on the baking sheet, about 1 inch apart. Bake until lightly golden brown, turning once, about 30 minutes.

6. Remove from the oven and let the granola balls cool completely. They will crisp up as they cool. Store in an airtight container at room temperature for up to 2 weeks.

Peanut Butter–Chocolate Energy Bites

MAKES 15 BITES

1 cup (packed) pitted Medjool dates

⅔ cup old-fashioned rolled oats, lightly toasted

2 ounces coarsely chopped bittersweet chocolate

1 tablespoon ground flaxseeds

3 tablespoons natural nut butter (peanut, almond, or cashew)

PER BITE: Calories **97**; Protein **2g**; Carbohydrates **14g**; Dietary Fiber **7g**; Sugar **8g**; Total Fat **4g**; Saturated Fat **1g**

Like candy with a conscience, these fiber-rich bites are great to have on hand any time that you need a bit of energy. Before or after a workout, or as a late afternoon pick-me-up, this delicious and balanced mix of protein-, fat-, and carb-fueled energy is sure to get you up and running.

1. Line a rimmed baking sheet with parchment paper or silicon baking mat.

2. Soak the dates in hot water for 15 minutes. Drain the dates, reserving ½ cup of the soaking liquid. Transfer the dates to a food processor and process until coarsely chopped and the mixture just starts to form a ball. Add a little of the reserved liquid if needed.

3. Add the oats, chocolate, flaxseeds, nut butter, and a few tablespoons of the soaking water to the dates and pulse or mix until combined. You want a mixture with small pieces, not something that is completely smooth.

4. Carefully roll the mixture into 1-inch balls using the warmth of your hands to mold them together. Put on the baking sheet and let set in the refrigerator for 30 minutes or freeze for 10 minutes. Keep in a zip-top plastic bag for up to a week in the refrigerator.

Peanut Butter–
Chocolate
Energy Bites

Raspberry–White
Peach Granola
Poppers

Mango Upside-Down Granola Bars with Macadamia and Coconut

MAKES 16 BARS

Nonstick cooking spray

16 thin dried mango slices

3 cups old-fashioned rolled oats

1 cup macadamia nuts, coarsely chopped

¼ cup sweetened shredded coconut

¼ cup coconut oil

1 teaspoon finely grated orange zest

¼ cup honey or agave syrup

¼ teaspoon ground allspice

¼ teaspoon fine sea salt

2 large egg whites

½ teaspoon pure vanilla extract

PER BAR: Calories **209**; Protein **4g**; Carbohydrates **22g**; Dietary Fiber **3g**; Sugar **5g**; Total Fat **12g**; Saturated Fat **5g**

I got the idea for this from a really fancy bakery I visited a few years ago in LA. I love the look of the finished bars, and you can't go wrong with the tropical combo of mango, macadamia, and coconut.

1. Preheat the oven to 300°F. Line an 18 × 13-inch rimmed baking sheet with parchment paper or a silicone baking mat. Spray the surface lightly with nonstick spray.

2. Soak the mango slices in hot water for 15 minutes. Drain and pat dry. Lay the mango slices onto the baking sheet in 4 rows of 4 slices each.

3. In a large bowl, mix together the oats, nuts, and coconut. In a small saucepan, combine the coconut oil, orange zest, honey, allspice, and salt and cook over low heat, whisking a few times, until melted. Remove from the heat and let cool for 5 minutes so that the egg white doesn't scramble when added.

4. In a small bowl, whisk together the egg whites and vanilla until fluffy. Stir into the oil mixture. Pour over the oat mixture and mix until combined.

5. Spread the oat mixture evenly over the mangos on the baking sheet and bake until lightly golden brown, 30 to 35 minutes. Transfer to a baking rack to cool completely. Cut into 16 bars. Store in a covered container for up to 1 week.

Apple Cider Caramel Apples with Walnuts

SERVES 6

Apple Cider Caramel

2 quarts unfiltered apple cider

1 teaspoon apple cider vinegar

Pinch of sea salt

2 tablespoons 2% Greek yogurt

3 apples, cored and cut into eighths (Granny Smith, Gala, or Fuji)

½ cup walnuts, toasted and finely chopped

PER SERVING: Calories **267**; Protein **2g**; Carbohydrates **52g**; Dietary Fiber **2g**; Sugar **43g**; Total Fat **6g**; Saturated Fat **1g**

What's not to love about an apple dipped in creamy caramel, rich with heavy cream and butter, then dredged in toasted nuts? Well, there might be *one* part of that equation not to love. Since I still look forward to getting my caramel apple fix each fall, I found a way to enjoy it without the guilt.

1. Make the caramel: Pour the cider into a medium nonreactive saucepan and bring to a boil over high heat. Reduce the heat to medium-low and simmer, stirring occasionally, until reduced to approximately 1½ cups, about 1 hour.

2. Whisk in the vinegar and salt and let cool to room temperature. Whisk in the yogurt. Cover and place in the refrigerator overnight to thicken slightly. The caramel will keep, covered in the refrigerator, for up to 3 days.

3. To serve, put the apple wedges in a bowl, drizzle with the caramel, and sprinkle with the nuts.

Roasted Edamame with Garlic Chips

SERVES 6

3 tablespoons olive oil

5 garlic cloves, sliced paper thin

Kosher salt and freshly ground black pepper

1 tablespoon grated lemon zest

1 (20-ounce) bag frozen edamame in pods, thawed

PER SERVING: Calories **123**; Protein **5g**; Carbohydrates **5g**; Dietary Fiber **2g**; Sugar **1g**; Total Fat **9g**; Saturated Fat **1g**

I have to give my respects to Nobu in Los Angeles for this recipe—it's one of my favorite appetizers there. Japanese restaurants typically serve edamame steamed and salted in the pod, and those are great, too, but this preparation is so much more noteworthy. Charring the soybeans inside their shell adds a great depth of flavor, and sweet and toasty garlic makes this virtuous snack irresistible.

1. Preheat the oven to 425°F. Line a rimmed baking sheet with parchment paper.

2. In a small sauté pan, heat the oil over low heat until the oil begins to shimmer. Add the garlic and cook, stirring occasionally, until lightly golden brown and crisp, about 3 minutes. Remove the garlic chips with a slotted spoon to a plate lined with paper towels and season with salt. Reserve the oil.

3. Put the edamame in a bowl, add the garlic oil, lemon zest, and salt and pepper to taste, and toss to coat. Spread the edamame in an even layer on the prepared baking sheet. Roast until the pods are charred and the beans are tender, 10 to 15 minutes.

4. Remove from the oven, transfer to a platter, and top with the garlic chips and additional salt, if needed.

Baked
Tortilla Chips

Baked
Pita Chips

Baked
Chile Cheese
Tortilla Chips

Baked
Taro Chips

Half a Dozen Baked Chip Recipes

Making your own chips is easy, quick, and much healthier and less expensive than buying bags of them. There's a world of flavor out there beyond fried potato chips. Here are a handful of easy recipes to ensure you have healthy chips ready for dipping any time. These recipes are also a great way to use up extra veggies and stale pita. Use a mandoline to slice veggies super-thin. Chips can be stored in an airtight container for up to two days.

Baked Tortilla Chips

SERVES 4

6 (6-inch) corn tortillas, cut into sixths

2 tablespoons canola oil

Kosher salt and freshly ground black pepper

PER SERVING: Calories **149**; Protein **2g**; Carbohydrates **18g**; Dietary Fiber **2g**; Sugar **0g**; Total Fat **8g**; Saturated Fat **1g**

Top these with ground cumin, ground coriander, or pure chile powder before baking, if desired.

1. Preheat the oven to 375°F.

2. Brush the tortillas on both sides with the oil and season with salt and pepper. Bake in an even layer on a rimmed baking sheet until lightly golden brown and crispy, about 10 minutes. Let cool completely.

VARIATION

Baked Chile Cheese Tortilla Chips

Nacho cheese–flavored tortilla chips were all the rage when I was a kid. Back then, I could polish off a large bag without a second thought. Today, I can't imagine it! But that doesn't mean cheesy, spiced chips have to remain a guilty pleasure of the past. Season and bake tortillas at home instead of frying them. Nutritional yeast tastes just like cheese and is a great source of B vitamins. Score!

In a small bowl, mix together 1 tablespoon ancho chile powder, 2 teaspoons nutritional yeast, 1 teaspoon ground cumin, ¼ teaspoon cayenne powder, ¼ teaspoon onion powder, and 1 teaspoon kosher salt. Sprinkle over the tortillas before baking.

Calories **153**; Protein **3g**; Carbohydrates **19g**

Baked Pita Chips

SERVES 8

8 whole-wheat pita breads, cut into sixths

2 tablespoons olive oil

Kosher salt and freshly ground black pepper

PER SERVING: Calories **204**; Protein **6g**; Carbohydrates **35g**; Dietary Fiber **5g**; Sugar **1g**; Total Fat **5g**; Saturated Fat **1g**

Top these with sesame seeds, poppy seeds, or finely chopped fresh herbs just before baking.

1. Preheat the oven to 400°F.

2. Brush the pita on both sides with the oil and season with salt and pepper. Bake in an even layer on a rimmed baking sheet until lightly golden brown and crispy, about 10 minutes. Let cool completely.

Baked Vegetable Chips

SERVES 6

1 medium beet, peeled and thinly sliced

1 large carrot, peeled and thinly sliced lengthwise

1 medium sweet potato, peeled and thinly sliced lengthwise

2 tablespoons olive oil in a sprayer

Kosher salt

Finely chopped fresh herbs, such as rosemary or thyme (optional)

PER SERVING: Calories **73**; Protein **1g**; Carbohydrates **7g**; Dietary Fiber **1g**; Sugar **4g**; Total Fat **5g**; Saturated Fat **1g**

1. Preheat the oven to 375°F.

2. Put the vegetables in a single layer on rimmed baking sheets, spray lightly with oil on both sides, and season with salt and herbs, if using. Bake the chips, turning once, until lightly golden brown and crisp, 10 to 12 minutes. Watch closely because they can burn and turn bitter.

3. Remove the pan to a baking rack and let cool completely before eating. The chips will crisp up more as they cool.

VARIATIONS

Baked Taro Chips

SERVES 4

Substitute 1 medium taro root (about 10 ounces), peeled and thinly sliced, for the vegetables, above, and use 1 tablespoon plus 1 teaspoon olive oil. Protein **2g**; Carbohydrates **5g**; Sugar **0g**

Baked Collard Chips

SERVES 2

Substitute 4 ounces chopped mixed hearty greens (collard, kale, mustard) for the vegetables and spray with 1 tablespoon olive oil. Calories **80**; Carbohydrates **3g**; Dietary Fiber **2g**; Sugar **0g**; Total Fat **7g**

Jicama with Chile, Salt, and Lime

SERVES 4

1 small head of jicama, peeled and cut into 3-inch-long by ¼-inch-thick strips

Grated zest and juice of 2 limes

1½ teaspoons kosher salt

1 teaspoon pure chile powder, such as ancho or New Mexico

PER SERVING: Calories **42**; Protein **1g**; Carbohydrates **10g**; Dietary Fiber **5g**; Sugar **3g**; Total Fat **0g**; Saturated Fat **0g**

You'll find roadside food vendors all over Mexico hawking this refreshing snack to the masses. Deftly seasoned and showered with lime juice, jicama, which is commonly described as having a flavor and texture akin to a cross between an apple and a potato, has it all: crunch, salt, spice, acid. It's also low-calorie to the point of practically being non-caloric. The next time you want to reach for a bag of crunchy potato chips, slice up some jicama instead.

Put the jicama in a large bowl, add the lime zest and juice, the salt, and chile powder, and toss to coat evenly. If you have time, cover and refrigerate until cold, about 1 hour. The jicama will keep, covered and stored in the refrigerator, for several days.

Flavored Popcorn

Popcorn is a healthy snack, although you wouldn't know it by reading the labels of the mass-produced varieties at the grocery store: toffee-coated, butter-drenched—the list goes on and on. Make it yourself instead. Now I know that the healthiest way is to air pop it, but I've always found that rather tasteless. A cup of air-popped popcorn has about 30 calories, while popcorn popped in a bit of fat has about 90—still healthy, still full of fiber, but much tastier. Here are a few of my favorite ways to get lots of flavor with few calories.

Perfectly Popped Corn

SERVES 4

3 tablespoons canola or coconut oil

⅔ cup popcorn kernels

Kosher salt

PER SERVING: Calories **216**; Protein **4g**; Carbohydrates **24g**; Dietary Fiber **4g**; Sugar **0g**; Total Fat **12g**; Saturated Fat **1g**

1. In a medium (3-quart) saucepan with a lid, heat the oil over medium-high heat until it begins to shimmer.

2. Add 4 kernels of the popcorn to the pan and once those kernels have all popped, add the remaining kernels in an even layer in the bottom of the pan and sprinkle 1 teaspoon salt evenly over the kernels. Cover the pan, remove the pan from the heat, and count to 30. Return the pan to the heat and once the kernels begin popping rapidly, start shaking the pan back and forth a few times and continue shaking occasionally until the popping begins to slow down considerably.

3. Immediately transfer the popcorn to a large bowl and season with additional salt, if desired. Or season as suggested on the following page.

Coconut-Curry Popcorn

SERVES 4

Scant ¼ cup sweetened shredded coconut

3 tablespoons coconut oil

Scant 1 teaspoon mild Madras curry powder

1 teaspoon sugar

Kosher salt (optional)

⅔ cup popcorn kernels

PER SERVING: Calories **251**; Protein **4g**; Carbohydrates **28g**; Dietary Fiber **4g**; Sugar **3g**; Total Fat **14g**; Saturated Fat **11g**

A touch sweet, a touch salty, and a whole lot delicious, this one is like an Indian-inspired kettle corn.

1. Heat a small nonstick sauté pan over low heat, add the coconut, and cook, stirring occasionally, until lightly golden brown. Let cool for 5 minutes, then transfer to a blender and blend until a fine powder forms.

2. In a 3-quart saucepan with a lid, heat the coconut oil over medium-high heat until the oil begins to shimmer. Stir in the curry powder and sugar and mix until they dissolve into the oil.

3. Use the curry oil to make popcorn as directed in Perfectly Popped Corn (opposite). Season the popcorn with the coconut powder and with additional salt, if desired.

VARIATION

Ancho Kettle Popcorn

We used to serve this at the bar at Mesa City, my offshoot of Mesa Grill on the Upper East Side of Manhattan, where we would literally go through buckets of it a night. As if the sweet and salty combination weren't enough, adding spice to the mix makes it positively addictive. Season Perfectly Popped Corn (opposite) with 1 tablespoon sugar and 1 tablespoon pure chile powder, such as ancho. Calories **225**; Protein **4g**; Carbohydrates **27g**; Dietary Fiber **4g**; Sugar **3g**; Total Fat **12g**; Saturated Fat **1g**

Three Hummus Recipes

Step away from the hummus in the refrigerated case at the supermarket! Those are fine in a pinch, but there's a whole world of flavor out there beyond even the garlic and roasted red pepper varieties. Here are a few of my favorites.

Spicy Black Bean–Lime Hummus

SERVES 6

1 tablespoon olive oil

2 garlic cloves, chopped

1 jalapeño pepper, chopped

1 teaspoon ground cumin

2 (15.5-ounce) cans black beans, drained, rinsed, and drained again

¼ cup tahini

2 teaspoons finely grated lime zest

2 tablespoons fresh lime juice

¼ cup chopped fresh cilantro, plus whole leaves for garnish

Kosher salt and freshly ground black pepper

¼ cup crumbled queso blanco

¼ cup Pickled Red Onions (page 32)

PER SERVING: Calories **280**; Protein **12g**; Carbohydrates **37g**; Dietary Fiber **8g**; Sugar **9g**; Total Fat **10g**; Saturated Fat **2g**

Enriched with tahini and a touch of olive oil, this limey black bean dip is creamier than most. The recipe calls for canned black beans for ease of preparation, but by all means make your own should you have the time (see page 47)! If you do, reserve some of the cooking water to use when processing the hummus for an even richer, fuller flavor.

1. In a small sauté pan, heat the olive oil over medium-low heat, add the garlic and jalapeño, and cook until soft, about 2 minutes. Add the cumin and cook 30 seconds longer.

2. In a medium bowl, lightly crush half of the beans with a potato masher or fork.

3. In a food processor, combine the remaining whole beans, the garlic and jalapeño, the tahini, ¼ cup water, the lime zest, and the lime juice and process until smooth. Add the cilantro, season with salt and black pepper to taste, and pulse a few times just to incorporate.

4. Scrape the hummus into a shallow bowl and fold in the crushed beans. Top with the cheese and pickled onions and garnish with cilantro leaves.

Roasted Carrot and Harissa Hummus with Dill

Spicy Black Bean–Lime Hummus

Avocado-Jalapeño Hummus

Avocado-Jalapeño Hummus

SERVES 6

1 tablespoon olive oil

2 garlic cloves, chopped

1 jalapeño pepper, chopped

1 teaspoon ground cumin

1 teaspoon ground coriander

1 (15.5-ounce) can chickpeas, drained, rinsed, and drained again

2 Hass avocados, peeled, pitted, and diced

Finely grated zest of 1 lime

Juice of 2 limes

¼ cup chopped fresh cilantro

Kosher salt and freshly ground black pepper

PER SERVING: Calories **191**; Protein **5g**; Carbohydrates **18g**; Dietary Fiber **6g**; Sugar **0g**; Total Fat **12g**; Saturated Fat **1g**

Call it fusion, call it a cross-cultural mash-up, call it whatever you like as long as it works—and whether you serve it with tortillas or pita, this Mexican–meets–Middle Eastern hummus dip *works*.

1. In a small sauté pan, heat the oil over medium heat until it shimmers. Add the garlic and jalapeño and cook until soft, about 2 minutes. Add the cumin and coriander and cook for 1 minute. Add ¼ cup water, bring to a simmer, and cook until thickened, about 1 minute longer. Set aside to cool.

2. In a medium bowl, lightly crush the chickpeas with a potato masher or fork.

3. Transfer the jalapeño mixture to a food processor and pulse a few times to coarsely chop. Add the avocados and pulse until smooth. Add the lime zest, lime juice, and cilantro and pulse to incorporate, leaving flecks of cilantro. Season with salt and black pepper.

4. Scrape the hummus into a shallow bowl and fold in the crushed chickpeas.

Roasted Carrot and Harissa Hummus with Dill

SERVES 6

4 medium carrots, peeled and cut into 1-inch pieces

2 tablespoons canola or olive oil

Kosher salt and freshly ground black pepper

2 (15.5-ounce) cans chickpeas, drained, rinsed, and drained again

2 garlic cloves, chopped

2 tablespoons harissa paste

¼ cup tahini

2 teaspoons finely grated lemon zest

Juice of 1 lemon

½ cup chopped fresh dill, plus whole sprigs for garnish

1 green onion, dark and pale green parts, sliced

PER SERVING: Calories **274**; Protein **9g**; Carbohydrates **31g**; Dietary Fiber **10g**; Sugar **3g**; Total Fat **13g**; Saturated Fat **1g**

One of the most popular dishes on the opening menu at my restaurant Gato was the spiced roasted carrots with harissa yogurt. Those sweet-earthy-spicy flavors, long paired in Moroccan cuisine, work together so well that this hummus was a natural next step. Roasted carrots bring more than flavor, including vitamin A and fiber.

1. Preheat the oven to 375°F.

2. On a rimmed baking sheet, toss the carrots in the oil and season with salt and pepper. Spread out in an even layer and roast until golden brown and soft, about 40 minutes. Remove from the oven and let cool for 10 minutes.

3. In a medium bowl, lightly crush half of the chickpeas with a potato masher or fork.

4. Transfer the carrots to a food processor. Add the remaining whole chickpeas, the garlic, harissa, tahini, ¼ cup water, and the lemon zest and juice and process until smooth. Add the dill, season with salt and pepper, and pulse a few times just to incorporate.

5. Scrape the hummus into a shallow bowl and fold in the crushed chickpeas. Garnish with the green onion and dill sprigs.

Four Iced Teas

Drinking flavored teas is a great way to stay hydrated without adding lots of extra sugar and calories. Serve these in tall glasses over ice from May through September, or even year-round if it means you can give up other sugary drinks.

Lime Rickey–Black Cherry Ice Green Tea

SERVES 4

8 black cherry green tea bags

1 tablespoon sugar

Zest of 2 limes in large peels

Juice of 2 limes

1 cup Bing cherries, pitted and halved, plus more for garnish, if desired

Ice cubes

4 lime wedges, for garnish

PER SERVING: Calories **12**; Protein **0g**; Carbohydrates **3g**; Dietary Fiber **0g**; Sugar **3g**; Total Fat **0g**; Saturated Fat **0g**

There aren't too many places out there mixing and pouring their own sodas these days, but for those of us who can remember the treat of a freshly mixed and poured lime rickey, this drink will take you back. This beverage combines the antioxidant power of green tea and the sweet summery taste of cherries with lots of fresh lime juice, of course.

1. In a medium saucepan, bring 6 cups cold water to a boil. Add the tea bags, sugar, and zest; cover, remove from the heat, and let steep for 5 minutes. Remove the tea bags and discard. Let the tea come to room temperature, then remove the zest, and discard.

2. Transfer the tea to a pitcher and add the lime juice and cherries. Cover and refrigerate until cold, at least 2 hours and up to 24 hours.

3. Serve over ice, garnishing each glass with a lime wedge and some cherries, if desired.

Sangria Tea
Sparkler

Lime Rickey–Black
Cherry Ice Green Tea

Watermelon
Mint Cooler

Sangria Tea Sparkler

SERVES 6

8 hibiscus tea bags

1 cup raspberries

1 cup sliced strawberries

1 small orange, halved, seeded, and thinly sliced

1 cup halved red grapes

2 cups orange sparkling water, very cold

PER SERVING: Calories **45**; Protein **1g**; Carbohydrates **11g**; Dietary Fiber **3g**; Sugar **8g**; Total Fat **0g**; Saturated Fat **0g**

This sangria gets its flamboyant pink color and fruity, softly floral flavor from iced hibiscus tea, not wine, making it the perfect nonalcoholic refreshment for your next warm-weather bash. Its only calories come from whole fruit, making this bright and sparkly beverage perfect for the calorie-conscious and nondrinkers, alike.

1. In a medium saucepan, bring 6 cups cold water to a boil and add the tea bags. Cover, remove from the heat, and let steep for 5 minutes. Remove the tea bags and discard. Let the tea cool for 5 minutes.

2. Transfer the tea to a pitcher and add the raspberries, strawberries, orange slices, and grapes. Cover and refrigerate until very cold and the flavors have melded, at least 4 hours and up to 24 hours.

3. Fill 6 glasses halfway with tea, add some of the fruit, and then top off with orange sparkling water.

Apple-Spice Tisane

SERVES 2

Peels from 8 apples

2 cinnamon sticks

3 whole cloves

Peel of 1 lemon

1 tablespoon fresh lemon juice

PER SERVING: Calories **0**; Protein **0g**; Carbohydrates **0g**; Dietary Fiber **0g**; Sugar **0g**; Total Fat **0g**; Saturated Fat **0g**

A tisane is an herbal tea, and here the "herb" is apple skins. This is a fantastic way to make something tasty out of a part of the fruit that would normally be tossed in the trash. This drink is soothing when warm and refreshing when iced.

1. In a medium saucepan, combine the apple peels, 2 cups water, the cinnamon sticks, cloves, and lemon peel. Bring to a boil and cook for 1 minute. Turn off the heat, cover, and let steep for 15 minutes.

2. Strain the tea. Reheat if desired. Add the lemon juice and divide between 2 mugs or glasses.

Watermelon Mint Cooler

SERVES 4

4 green tea bags

4 mint tea bags

¼ cup fresh mint

4 cups 1-inch cubed seedless watermelon

PER SERVING: Calories **55**; Protein **0g**; Carbohydrates **14g**; Dietary Fiber **1g**; Sugar **13g**; Total Fat **0g**; Saturated Fat **0g**

Watermelon and mint are such a phenomenal combination—the herb really perks up the fruit's juicy sweetness. Iced green tea is super-thirst-quenching, and the combination of all parts is incredibly refreshing. Cubed watermelon infuses the tea with its natural sweetness, no extra sugar needed!

1. In a medium saucepan, bring 6 cups cold water to a boil and add both kinds of tea bags. Cover, remove from the heat, and let steep for 5 minutes. Remove the tea bags and discard. Let the tea cool for 5 minutes.

2. Pour the tea into a pitcher, add the mint, cover, and refrigerate until cold and the flavors have melded, at least 4 hours and up to 24 hours.

3. Arrange the watermelon cubes in a single layer on a rimmed baking sheet and freeze until firm, at least 1 hour.

4. Divide the watermelon cubes among 4 glasses and top with the tea.

LUNCH

Tomato Bread with Green Eggs and Ham

SERVES 4

Tomato Bread

1 whole-wheat baguette, sliced on the bias into twelve 1-inch slices

2 garlic cloves, cut in half crosswise

2 tablespoons extra-virgin olive oil

Kosher salt and freshly ground black pepper

2 large very ripe beefsteak tomatoes

Green Eggs

1 tablespoon olive oil

1 tablespoon unsalted butter

6 large eggs

2 large egg whites

Kosher salt and freshly ground black pepper

2 tablespoons chopped fresh flat-leaf parsley

1 tablespoon finely chopped fresh chives, plus more for garnish

2 teaspoons finely chopped fresh tarragon

1 ounce grated Manchego cheese

6 paper-thin slices of Serrano ham, cut in half

PER SERVING: Calories **451**; Protein **22g**; Carbohydrates **33g**; Dietary Fiber **1g**; Sugar **5g**; Total Fat **25g**; Saturated Fat **8g**

This is a perfect example of a dish where fresh flavors please the palate and satisfy: thin slices of salty rich ham, fresh green herbs, sweet tomatoes, creamy eggs, and crunchy toast. You may see Manchego cheese and Serrano ham and think, how is this healthy? Small amounts add big flavor, and "everything in moderation" is my mantra.

1. Start the tomato bread: Preheat the oven to 425°F.

2. Arrange the bread in a single layer on a rimmed baking sheet and bake until crisp on the outside but still chewy on the inside, about 7 minutes. Remove from the oven and immediately rub the garlic over the top of each slice, drizzle with the extra-virgin olive oil, and season with salt and pepper.

3. While the bread is toasting, grate the tomatoes on a grater set over a bowl and season with salt.

4. Cook the eggs: In a large nonstick sauté pan, heat the olive oil and butter over medium heat until the mixture begins to shimmer.

5. In a medium bowl, whisk together the eggs and whites until light and fluffy. Season with salt and pepper. Transfer the mixture to the pan and cook, stirring with a rubber spatula, until large curds form and the mixture is just set, about 3 minutes. Remove the pan from the heat and stir in the herbs and cheese.

6. Divide the tomato mixture among the slices of bread, top with the eggs, and then top each slice with half a slice of the ham. Garnish with chives.

Pickled Egg Niçoise Tartine

SERVES 2

½ small red onion, thinly sliced

¼ cup chopped pitted Niçoise olives

1 (6.7-ounce) jar best-quality tuna packed in olive oil, drained well

2 tablespoons of the egg pickling liquid plus 2 Saffron Pickled Eggs (recipe follows), thinly sliced

Kosher salt and ground black pepper

4 slices seeded bread, ¼ inch thick

4 teaspoons 2% Greek yogurt

2 plum tomatoes, thinly sliced

2 tablespoons chopped fresh flat-leaf parsley, plus whole leaves for garnish

PER SERVING (INCLUDES EGGS): Calories **443**; Protein **37g**; Carbohydrates **34g**; Dietary Fiber **4g**; Sugar **9g**; Total Fat **17g**; Saturated Fat **4g**

A tartine is an elegant open-faced sandwich, perfect for sharing with lunch guests or enjoying by yourself. Since the name is French, how about a topping inspired by the famously flavorful salade Niçoise to match? If you don't want to make pickled eggs, regular hard-cooked eggs are fine, too. In that case, add a few tablespoons of red or white wine vinegar to the tuna salad to bring out all of the flavors.

1. In a medium bowl, combine the onion, olives, tuna, and pickling liquid and season with salt and pepper. Let sit at room temperature for 15 minutes or cover and refrigerate for up to 24 hours before serving.

2. Toast the bread until lightly golden brown on both sides. Spread the top side of each piece with yogurt and top with 2 slices of tomato; season with salt and pepper. Stir the chopped parsley into the tuna salad and divide among the toasts and top with slices of egg. Garnish with parsley leaves.

Saffron Pickled Eggs

MAKES 6

1½ cups white wine vinegar

2 garlic cloves

¼ teaspoon saffron threads

1 tablespoon black peppercorns

1 tablespoon caraway seeds

1 teaspoon fennel seeds

1 tablespoon kosher salt

¼ cup cane sugar

6 hard-cooked eggs, peeled

1. In a medium saucepan, combine the vinegar, 1 cup water, the garlic, saffron, peppercorns, caraway, fennel, salt, and sugar. Bring to a boil, reduce to a simmer, and cook for 2 minutes or until the sugar has dissolved and the saffron threads have thoroughly bloomed. Remove from the heat and allow to cool for 5 minutes.

2. Place the peeled eggs into a large heat-proof bowl or jar and pour the warm pickling liquid over them until completely submerged. Cover with plastic wrap or a tight-fitting lid and refrigerate for 24 to 48 hours. Pickled eggs, if stored in the refrigerator, should keep for approximately 3 weeks.

PER SERVING: Calories **78**; Protein **6g**; Carbohydrates **1g**; Dietary Fiber **0g**; Sugar **1g**; Total Fat **5g**; Saturated Fat **2g**

Salmon Gyro with Roasted Tomato–Mustard Seed Tzatziki

SERVES 4

2 plum tomatoes, halved and seeded

1 tablespoon canola oil

Kosher salt and freshly ground black pepper

1 cup Tzatziki (page 24) or store-bought

2 tablespoons country-style Dijon mustard (with seeds)

4 Yogurt Flatbread (page 119) or store-bought flatbread

4 (5-ounce) salmon fillets, grilled or pan-seared (see page 49)

½ recipe Shredded Greens with Feta, Dill, and Green Onion (page 135)

PER SERVING: Calories **631**; Protein **39g**; Carbohydrates **32g**; Dietary Fiber **4g**; Sugar **7g**; Total Fat **38g**; Saturated Fat **7g**

This is equally as delicious with grilled chicken or shrimp in place of the salmon. You can use store-bought flatbread if you are short on time, or wrap it in butter lettuce leaves for a no-carb, gluten-free version.

1. Preheat the oven to 325°F.

2. Brush the tomatoes with the oil on both sides and season with salt and pepper. Roast in a small ovenproof dish until the tomatoes are soft and the liquid has evaporated. Transfer to a cutting board and finely chop.

3. Put the tzatziki in a small bowl and stir in the mustard and chopped tomatoes.

4. Heat the flatbreads on both sides on the grill or wrap in foil and heat in the oven for 10 minutes.

5. Lay the flatbreads on a level surface and spread the tzatziki over them. Slice the salmon and lay it on top of the sauce, top with some of the salad, roll each flatbread tightly, and slice in half crosswise.

Yogurt Flatbread

MAKES 8

1 cup whole-wheat flour

1 cup unbleached all-purpose flour

1 tablespoon baking powder

1 teaspoon kosher salt

1 cup 2% Greek yogurt

Nonstick cooking spray

¼ cup extra-virgin olive oil

PER FLATBREAD: Calories **191**;
Protein **6g**; Carbohydrates **24g**;
Dietary Fiber **2g**; Sugar **2g**;
Total Fat **8g**; Saturated Fat **1g**

Homemade bread makes any meal seem special, and this tangy, chewy flatbread does just that in practically no time at all. Three minutes of kneading and fifteen minutes of proofing are all it takes to get this dough ready. I love it as part of a mezze platter; it's the perfect delivery vehicle for swipes of thick yogurt dips and creamy hummus.

1. In a small bowl, whisk together the flours, baking powder, and salt. In a medium bowl, whisk together the yogurt and ¼ cup water until smooth. Add the flour mixture and mix until combined. Turn out onto a lightly floured surface and gently knead the dough until soft and smooth, about 3 minutes.

2. Put in a clean bowl, cover with plastic wrap, and let rest for 15 minutes. Divide into 8 equal portions, roll into balls, and keep covered with plastic wrap or a clean cloth.

3. Heat an 8-inch nonstick or cast-iron pan over medium heat. Spray with nonstick spray. Roll one ball into a 5-inch circle. Brush the top with a little of the oil and put in the pan, oil side down. Cook until the bottom is evenly golden brown, about 4 minutes. Brush the top of the flatbread with more oil, flip it over, and continue cooking until the bottom is golden brown, about 3 minutes longer. Keep warm in towels. Repeat with the remaining balls of dough.

VARIATIONS

Seeded Flatbread

Brush the tops of the rolled dough with a touch of oil; sprinkle each with ¼ teaspoon sesame seeds or poppy seeds. Calories **192**

Garlic Flatbread

Brush tops with 1 teaspoon garlic oil. Calories **196**; Total Fat **9g**; Saturated Fat **2g**

Sea Salt Flatbread

Brush tops with 1 teaspoon oil and sprinkle each with ½ teaspoon coarse sea salt. Calories **196**; Total Fat **9g**; Saturated Fat **2g**

Cuban Fish Tacos with Mojo Red Cabbage Slaw

SERVES 6

Slaw

3 tablespoons aged sherry vinegar

2 tablespoons orange marmalade

Finely grated zest and juice of 1 lime

Few dashes of habanero hot sauce

2 garlic cloves, smashed and chopped to a paste

Kosher salt and freshly ground black pepper

½ small head of red cabbage, finely shredded

1 small ripe mango, peeled, pitted, and julienned

2 green onions, dark and pale green parts, thinly sliced

Tacos

1 teaspoon ground cumin

1 teaspoon kosher salt

¼ teaspoon garlic powder

¼ teaspoon onion powder

¼ teaspoon dried oregano

¼ teaspoon freshly ground black pepper

1½ pounds skinless flaky white fish fillets, such as mahimahi or red snapper

2 tablespoons olive oil

1 lime, halved

12 (6-inch) white or yellow corn tortillas, warmed in foil

PER SERVING: Calories **314**; Protein **25g**; Carbohydrates **39g**; Dietary Fiber **4g**; Sugar **12g**; Total Fat **7g**; Saturated Fat **1g**

One of my favorite meals to usher in summer is a platter of fish tacos; they're such a warm-weather dish to me. Most of the time I turn to California or Mexico for inspiration, but this recipe looks instead to the official Sunshine State, Florida, and its vibrant Cuban population in Miami. A time-honored and enticingly flavorful blend of spices known as sazón completa makes a savory spice rub for flaky white fish that gets topped with a healthy slaw of red cabbage, sweet mango, and fresh green onion for texture. The sweet-and-sour dressing of orange marmalade and sherry vinegar is a total nod to the sour orange mojo of classic Cuban cuisine.

1. Make the slaw: In a large bowl, whisk together the vinegar, marmalade, lime zest and juice, hot sauce, and garlic and season with salt and pepper. Let sit at room temperature for 10 minutes.

2. Add the red cabbage, mango, and green onions, season again with salt and pepper, and toss to coat. Cover and refrigerate for at least 30 minutes and up to 4 hours.

3. Make the tacos: In a small bowl, combine the cumin, salt, garlic powder, onion powder, oregano, and pepper.

4. Brush the fish with oil on both sides and season the top with the spice rub. Let sit at room temperature for 15 minutes.

5. Heat a grill pan or nonstick sauté pan over high heat. Cook the fish, rub side down, until golden brown and slightly charred, about 5 minutes. Turn it over and continue cooking until cooked through, 5 minutes more. Remove the fish to a cutting board, squeeze lime over, and let rest for 5 minutes before flaking.

6. Serve the fish in warm tortillas topped with some of the slaw.

Greek Fish Tacos with Grape Tomato Relish and Tzatziki Crema

SERVES 6

Grape Tomato Relish

1 pint grape tomatoes, halved

½ small red onion, thinly sliced

¼ cup chopped pitted kalamata olives

2 tablespoons red wine vinegar

2 tablespoons extra-virgin olive oil

Kosher salt and freshly ground black pepper

2 tablespoons finely chopped fresh flat-leaf parsley

1 teaspoon finely chopped fresh oregano

Fish

¼ cup olive oil

2 tablespoons fresh oregano

Kosher salt and freshly ground black pepper

1½ pounds skinless flaky white fish fillets, such as striped bass or snapper

1 lemon, halved

12 (6-inch) flour tortillas, warmed in foil

¾ cup Tzatziki (page 24) or store-bought

PER SERVING (INCLUDES TZATZIKI): Calories **480**; Protein **27g**; Carbohydrates **40g**; Dietary Fiber **3g**; Sugar **4g**; Total Fat **23g**; Saturated Fat **4g**

This is a really fun recipe: It puts a Greek spin on fish tacos. Simply grilled white fish and tortillas are the common denominators here, but a traditional Mexican salsa goes Greek with oregano, parsley, and briny olives. The crema is replaced with garlicky cucumber-and-yogurt tzatziki instead.

1. Make the tomato relish: In a medium bowl, combine the tomatoes, onion, olives, vinegar, and extra-virgin olive oil and season with salt and pepper. Let sit at room temperature for at least 15 minutes and up to 4 hours. Stir in the herbs just before serving.

2. Marinate the fish: In a blender, combine the olive oil and oregano, season with salt and pepper, and puree until smooth. Put the fish in a baking dish, pour the marinade over, turn to coat, and let sit at room temperature for 15 minutes.

3. Heat a grill pan or a nonstick sauté pan over high heat. Remove the fish from the marinade and season on both sides with salt and pepper. Cook on both sides until golden brown and just cooked through, about 5 minutes per side. Remove to a cutting board, squeeze lemon over, and let rest for 5 minutes before flaking.

4. Serve the fish in warm tortillas topped with some of the relish. Add a large dollop of tzatziki to each.

Peruvian Ceviche with Popcorn

SERVES 4

½ cup fresh lime juice

½ cup fresh lemon juice

2 tablespoons rice wine vinegar

1 tablespoon aji amarillo paste

1 teaspoon ground turmeric

¼ cup bottled clam juice

1 tablespoon finely grated peeled
   fresh ginger

Kosher salt and freshly ground black
   pepper

½ pound shrimp, peeled, deveined,
   and blanched

½ pound calamari, cut into rings and
   blanched

1 yellow tomato, seeded and diced

1 small yellow bell pepper, seeded
   and diced

2 tablespoons finely chopped fresh
   chives

Perfectly Popped Corn (page 100)

PER SERVING: Calories **201**;
Protein **22g**; Carbohydrates **18g**;
Dietary Fiber **2g**; Sugar **3g**;
Total Fat **5g**; Saturated Fat **1g**

I could eat ceviche every day and never get tired of it. Always clean and refreshing, it's a great protein-packed light meal. There are so many different fish and shellfish to use, so many vegetables and fruits to add, and so many ways to dress them. This particular ceviche is an homage to its birthplace, Peru, and includes one the country's most popular chiles, aji amarillo. It adds a bright complex flavor, as well as its distinctive yellow-orange color. If you can't find the paste, a pinch of red crushed pepper flakes can be substituted. Flavored Popcorn (pages 100–101) would be a fun garnish, adding a nice bit of crunch to the dish.

1. In a nonreactive bowl, whisk together the citrus juices, vinegar, aji amarillo, turmeric, clam juice, ginger, and a pinch each of salt and black pepper.

2. Add the shrimp, calamari, tomato, and bell pepper, cover, and refrigerate for 1 hour.

3. To serve, top with the chives and popcorn.

Yellowtail Poke with Mizuna and Taro Chips

SERVES 4

2 cups fresh pineapple juice

1-inch piece of peeled fresh ginger

1 garlic clove, smashed

2 tablespoons low-sodium tamari

2 tablespoons fresh lime juice

1 teaspoon toasted sesame oil

1 Thai chile, finely diced

1¼ pounds fresh yellowtail, cut into fine dice

4 ounces mizuna (or mixed greens)

Lime wedges, for garnish

Baked Taro Chips (page 98)

PER SERVING: Calories **374**; Protein **37g**; Carbohydrates **24g**; Dietary Fiber **2g**; Sugar **17g**; Total Fat **14g**; Saturated Fat **3g**

Poke (pronounced po-kay) is a traditional Hawaiian dish that typically calls for raw tuna or salmon that has been marinated in sweet and spicy flavors. As when making any raw fish dish, you must have the freshest fish possible, so find a reputable fishmonger in your area. I love using yellowtail for this dish, but if you can't find it, fresh tuna or salmon will work nicely, too.

1. In a small nonreactive saucepan, combine the pineapple juice, ginger, and garlic and boil over high heat, stirring occasionally, until reduced to ½ cup, about 30 minutes. Discard the ginger and garlic and pour the reduced juice into a large bowl. Whisk in the tamari, lime juice, and sesame oil. Reserve 2 tablespoons of the dressing for the mizuna.

2. Add the fish to the dressing and toss to coat. Put the mizuna in a large bowl, add the reserved dressing, and toss to coat. Divide the greens among 4 large plates and top with the poke. Garnish with lime wedges and taro chips.

Sweet Potato and Black Bean Tacos with Pickled Green Onions

SERVES 4

2 medium sweet potatoes, peeled and cut into 1-inch dice

2 tablespoons olive oil

½ teaspoon ground cinnamon, preferably Ceylon

Kosher salt and freshly ground black pepper

1 cup canned black beans, rinsed, drained, and rinsed again

8 (6-inch) corn tortillas, warmed in foil

¼ cup Pickled Green Onions (page 34)

½ cup Almond Salsa (recipe follows)

PER SERVING (INCLUDES SALSA): Calories **363**; Protein **9g**; Carbohydrates **54g**; Dietary Fiber **9g**; Sugar **8g**; Total Fat **13g**; Saturated Fat **2g**

This recipe is a perfect example of how healthy Mexican food can be. Typically, we think of it as lots of cheese and lard—but that's not always the case. Pickled vegetables play a big role in Latin cuisine, and not only are they crunchy but they're also fat-free and low in calories. Sweet potatoes are full of vitamin C, potassium, beta carotene, and fiber. The almond salsa is a cross between a romesco sauce and a salsa verde, with nuts helping to thicken and add a dose of protein. It's pretty addictive and can be served on its own as a dip for veggies or chips.

1. Preheat the oven to 425°F.

2. On a rimmed baking sheet, toss the sweet potatoes with the oil and season with the cinnamon and salt and pepper to taste. Spread in an even layer on the baking sheet and roast, turning once, until soft and lightly golden brown, about 35 minutes. During the last 5 minutes of roasting, add the black beans to the sweet potatoes to heat through.

3. Spread some of the salsa into the center of each tortilla, add some of the potato-bean mixture, and top with pickled green onions and more almond salsa. Roll and eat.

Almond Salsa

MAKES 1½ CUPS

1 pound tomatillos, husks removed, scrubbed, and cut into large dice

2 plum tomatoes, halved

1 small red onion, chopped

1 garlic clove, smashed

2 tablespoons olive oil

Kosher salt and freshly ground black pepper

2 piquillo peppers, chopped

¼ cup lightly toasted slivered almonds

¼ teaspoon chile de árbol powder

¼ cup chopped fresh cilantro

1 tablespoon aged sherry vinegar or red wine vinegar

1. Preheat the oven to 400°F. On a rimmed baking sheet, toss the tomatillos, tomatoes, onion, and garlic with the oil and season with salt and black pepper. Spread on the baking sheet in an even layer and roast until lightly golden brown and soft, about 30 minutes.

2. Transfer the mixture to a food processor, add the piquillo peppers, almonds, and chile de árbol, and pulse until smooth. Add the cilantro and pulse a few times to incorporate. Transfer to a bowl, stir in the vinegar, and let come to room temperature.

PER 2 TABLESPOONS:
Calories **55**; Protein **1g**; Carbohydrates **4g**; Dietary Fiber **1g**; Sugar **1g**; Total Fat **4g**; Saturated Fat **0g**

Roasted Carrot Hummus Salad with Cucumber Vinaigrette and Pita Chips

SERVES 4

Cucumber Vinaigrette

1 small cucumber, peeled, seeded, and chopped

3 tablespoons red wine vinegar

2 tablespoons chopped fresh chives

2 tablespoons chopped fresh flat-leaf parsley

1 tablespoon 2% Greek yogurt

2 teaspoons Dijon mustard

2 teaspoons prepared horseradish, drained

¼ cup extra-virgin olive oil

Kosher salt and freshly ground black pepper

Salad

4 ounces spinach leaves, stemmed and finely shredded

4 ounces romaine hearts, shredded

2 plum tomatoes, seeded and diced

1 small red onion, halved and thinly sliced

1 cup Roasted Carrot and Harissa Hummus with Dill (page 105)

4 ounces Greek feta, crumbled

1 tablespoon white sesame seeds, toasted (see Note page 28)

¼ recipe Baked Pita Chips (page 98; cut pita crosswise into thin strips before baking)

PER SERVING: Calories **441**; Protein **12g**; Carbohydrates **37g**; Dietary Fiber **8g**; Sugar **6g**; Total Fat **28g**; Saturated Fat **7g**

I'm not blind to the allure of a meal in a bowl: Grain bowls, yogurt bowls, they're all making the rounds! This salad is somewhere along those lines, and I liken it to a mezze bowl. Anchored by a hearty scoop of carrot hummus, the combo of crunchy romaine lettuce hearts, earthy spinach, and sharp red onion is colorful and fresh, and it's only improved by being punctuated with salty cubes of briny feta cheese. The dressing is something new for me; looking for a way to get more flavor into my vinaigrettes without adding extra fat and calories, I tried a base of fresh cucumber juice paired with just enough horseradish to keep you on your toes. It's a winner.

1. Make the vinaigrette: In a blender, combine the cucumber, vinegar, chives, parsley, yogurt, mustard, horseradish, and oil and blend until smooth. Season with salt and pepper to taste.

2. Toss the salad: In a large bowl, combine the spinach, romaine, tomatoes, and onion. Toss with some of the vinaigrette and transfer to shallow bowls. Top each with ¼ cup of the hummus, a sprinkling of feta, and some sesame seeds; drizzle with more of the dressing. Serve topped with the pita chips.

Harvest Salad with Pomegranate Mustard Vinaigrette

SERVES 6

Pomegranate Mustard Vinaigrette

2 tablespoons pomegranate molasses

3 tablespoons red wine vinegar

1 teaspoon finely grated orange zest

1 teaspoon Dijon mustard

Kosher salt and freshly ground black pepper

½ cup extra-virgin olive oil

Salad

4 ounces baby spinach

1 bunch of dinosaur (lacinato) kale, stemmed and shredded

¼ cup dried cranberries

2 cups diced roasted butternut squash

½ cup toasted walnuts, chopped

1 cup cooked Wild Rice (page 46)

2 ounces soft goat cheese, crumbled

1 large Asian pear, pear, or apple, cored and thinly sliced

2 tablespoons roasted sunflower seeds

Kosher salt and freshly ground black pepper

PER SERVING: Calories **411**; Protein **7g**; Carbohydrates **32g**; Dietary Fiber **6g**; Sugar **12g**; Total Fat **29g**; Saturated Fat **5g**

This salad makes an appearance on the menu at Bar Americain each fall and is always a best seller. Everything in it is healthy and it is the perfect combination of sweet, sour, and crunchy.

1. Make the vinaigrette: In a medium bowl, whisk together the pomegranate molasses, vinegar, orange zest, and mustard and season with salt and pepper. Slowly drizzle in the oil until emulsified.

2. Toss the salad: In a large bowl, mix together the spinach, kale, cranberries, butternut squash, walnuts, wild rice, goat cheese, pear, and sunflower seeds. Toss with the dressing and season with salt and pepper.

Shrimp Pad Thai Salad

SERVES 4

Spicy Nut Dressing

¼ cup rice wine vinegar

Juice of 1 lime

1 heaping tablespoon natural peanut, almond, or cashew butter

2 teaspoons chile-garlic sauce (such as Sriracha)

½ cup canola oil

Kosher salt and freshly ground black pepper

Salad

4 ounces baby arugula

2 ounces mesclun greens

1 large carrot, peeled and shredded

¼ small head of red cabbage, finely shredded

1 medium English cucumber, diced

2 ounces bean sprouts

¼ cup torn fresh basil

Kosher salt and freshly ground black pepper

12 large shrimp, grilled or pan-seared (see page 49)

¼ cup chopped toasted cashews, peanuts, or almonds

PER SERVING: Calories **409**; Protein **10g**; Carbohydrates **15g**; Dietary Fiber **4g**; Sugar **5g**; Total Fat **35g**; Saturated Fat **2g**

Pad thai, the peanut- and egg-laden Thai noodle dish, is a carb-lover's dream, but man, is it caloric! But I love all those nutty, sweet, spicy, and savory flavors. This salad is the healthy and delicious answer to all your cravings. It's fresh, crunchy, full of flavor, and loaded with lean protein—totally satisfying.

1. Make the dressing: In a blender, combine the vinegar, lime juice, nut butter, chile sauce, oil, and ½ cup water, season with salt and pepper, and blend until smooth.

2. Toss the salad: In a large bowl, mix together the greens, carrot, cabbage, cucumber, bean sprouts, and basil, add some of the dressing, and toss to coat. Season with salt and pepper. Transfer to a platter and top with the shrimp, additional dressing, and the chopped nuts.

Greek Salad with Herbed Tofu "Feta"

SERVES 4

Herbed Tofu

1 (10-ounce) block firm tofu

¼ cup fresh lemon juice

¼ cup white vinegar

1 teaspoon kosher salt

1 tablespoon finely chopped fresh oregano

1 tablespoon finely chopped fresh flat-leaf parsley, plus whole leaves for garnish

Greek Salad

4 large beefsteak tomatoes, seeded and diced

1 English cucumber, halved, seeded, and cut into 1-inch dice

½ red onion, thinly sliced

½ cup kalamata olives, pitted and halved

Juice of ½ lemon

¼ cup extra-virgin olive oil, preferably Greek

Kosher salt and freshly ground black pepper

PER SERVING: Calories **249**; Protein **6g**; Carbohydrates **15g**; Dietary Fiber **3g**; Sugar **7g**; Total Fat **19g**; Saturated Fat **3g**

There is no lettuce in "real" Greek salad, known as horiatiki or farmer's salad, only impeccably ripe tomatoes, cucumbers, and olives alongside shards of glorious, briny feta and a generous dose of extra-virgin olive oil. It's not exactly unhealthy, but replacing the real creamy feta with feta-esque tofu pushes the salad to the top of the fit list, cutting fat and adding tons of protein.

1. Prep the tofu: Line a plate with several layer of paper towels. Put the tofu on the towels and top with several paper towels. Put a second plate on top of the tofu and weight it down with heavy cans. Transfer to the refrigerator to drain for at least 2 hours and up to 24 hours.

2. In a medium bowl, whisk together the lemon juice, vinegar, ¼ cup water, the salt, oregano, and parsley. Thinly slice the tofu, add to the bowl, and toss to coat. Cover and refrigerate for at least 2 hours and up to 8 hours. Gently stir the mixture a few times during the marinating process.

3. Serve the salad: In a large bowl, combine the tomatoes, cucumber, onion, and olives. Toss with the lemon juice and oil and season with salt and pepper. Top with the marinated tofu, and garnish with parsley leaves.

Mustard-Marinated Kale Salad with Caramelized Onion and Spicy Chickpeas

SERVES 4

Does the world really need yet another kale salad? Yes. Kale is just so good and so good for you (full of calcium and vitamins A, K, and C) that I couldn't resist. Plus, this salad couldn't be simpler or more satisfying. Let the dressed kale sit at room temperature or in the refrigerator for a few hours before you serve it for a softer, gentler salad, or serve it right away and enjoy it in its naturally crunchy state.

Caramelized Onion

2 tablespoons olive oil

1 large sweet onion, halved and thinly sliced

¼ cup apple cider vinegar

Kosher salt and freshly ground black pepper

Kale Salad

½ teaspoon yellow mustard seeds

3 tablespoons apple cider vinegar

2 teaspoons Dijon mustard

Kosher salt and freshly ground black pepper

3 tablespoons extra-virgin olive oil

6 ounces curly kale, stemmed, leaves finely shredded

1 cup Roasted Chickpeas (page 86), seasoned with paprika and ground coriander

PER SERVING: Calories **284**; Protein **5g**; Carbohydrates **20g**; Dietary Fiber **5g**; Sugar **4g**; Total Fat **21g**; Saturated Fat **3g**

1. Caramelize the onion: In a large nonstick sauté pan, heat the oil over medium heat until it begins to shimmer. Add the onion and cook, slowly, until the onion begins to caramelize and turn lightly golden brown, about 20 minutes. Add the vinegar and continue cooking until the onion is deep golden brown, 10 minutes. Season with salt and pepper.

2. Start the salad: Heat a small pan over low heat, add the mustard seeds, and cook, shaking the pan a few times, until toasted lightly, about 3 minutes. Remove and let cool slightly.

3. In a large bowl, whisk together the vinegar, mustard, and salt and pepper to taste. Add the oil slowly, whisking to emulsify. Stir in the mustard seeds. Add the kale and toss with tongs until completely dressed. Let sit at room temperature for at least 15 minutes.

4. Transfer to a platter and top with the caramelized onion and the roasted chickpeas.

Saffron Bulgur Salad with Goat Cheese and Marcona Almond Dressing

SERVES 6

Roasted Tomatoes

1 pint cherry tomatoes, halved

1 tablespoon olive oil

Kosher salt and freshly ground black pepper

1 teaspoon finely chopped fresh thyme

Saffron Bulgur

3 cups Best Vegetable Stock (page 140) or low-sodium store-bought

Pinch of saffron threads

2 tablespoons olive oil

1 small red onion, finely diced

1½ cups bulgur

1 teaspoon kosher salt

⅛ teaspoon freshly ground black pepper

Marcona Almond Dressing (recipe follows)

¼ cup chopped fresh flat-leaf parsley

4 ounces soft goat cheese, crumbled

2 tablespoons Marcona almonds, toasted

PER SERVING (INCLUDES DRESSING): Calories **482**; Protein **11g**; Carbohydrates **32g**; Dietary Fiber **8g**; Sugar **3g**; Total Fat **35g**; Saturated Fat **7g**

I love the flavors of the Mediterranean. Saffron, sherry vinegar, smoked paprika, and buttery Marcona almonds are some of my favorite ingredients. They also pair really well with chewy, nutty bulgur, a staple grain in the cuisines of neighboring North Africa and the Arabian Peninsula. Tangy goat cheese helps to bind the salad's various components, as does the dressing, which has a natural sweetness gained from the extra-sweet, stubby almonds.

1. Roast the tomatoes: Preheat the oven to 250°F.

2. Spread the tomatoes on a rimmed baking sheet lined with parchment paper, drizzle with the oil, and season with salt and pepper and the thyme. Roast the tomatoes until shriveled and dry but still slightly juicy, about 3 hours (depending on how big the tomatoes are). The tomatoes can be stored covered with extra-virgin olive oil in a container with a tight-fitting lid in the refrigerator for up to 2 days.

3. Cook the bulgur: In a medium saucepan, combine the broth and saffron and bring to a boil over high heat. Remove from the heat, cover the pan, and let steep for 5 minutes.

4. In another medium saucepan, heat the oil over high heat. Add the onion and cook until soft, about 4 minutes. Stir in the bulgur and cook for 1 minute. Add the saffron broth, season with the salt and pepper, and bring to a boil. Reduce the heat, cover, and simmer until tender, 12 to 15 minutes. Drain off any excess liquid and transfer the bulgur to a large bowl.

5. Add half of the dressing, the tomatoes, and the parsley. Let sit at room temperature for 30 minutes before serving.

6. Add the goat cheese just before serving. Drizzle with additional dressing and garnish with the almonds.

Marcona Almond Dressing

MAKES ABOUT 1 CUP

¼ cup Marcona almonds

¼ cup aged sherry vinegar

⅛ teaspoon smoked sweet Spanish paprika

¼ teaspoon kosher salt

⅛ teaspoon freshly ground black pepper

½ cup extra-virgin olive oil

1. Preheat the oven to 325°F.

2. Spread the almonds on a rimmed baking sheet and roast, turning once, until lightly golden brown, about 8 minutes. Remove from the oven and let cool before finely chopping.

3. In a medium bowl, whisk together the vinegar, paprika, salt, and pepper. Slowly whisk in the oil until emulsified. Stir in the almonds and let sit at room temperature for at least 30 minutes and up to 1 hour to allow the flavors to meld.

PER 2 TABLESPOONS: Calories **149**; Protein **1g**; Carbohydrates **1g**; Dietary Fiber **0g**; Sugar **0g**; Total Fat **16g**; Saturated Fat **2g**

Shredded Greens with Feta, Dill, and Green Onion

SERVES 4

1 teaspoon finely grated lemon zest

3 tablespoons fresh lemon juice

1 tablespoon red wine vinegar

Kosher salt and ground black pepper

½ cup extra-virgin olive oil

1 small head of romaine, core removed, finely shredded

4 ounces spinach, stems removed, cut into chiffonade or finely shredded

2 large green onions, dark and pale green parts, halved lengthwise and thinly sliced crosswise

¼ cup chopped fresh dill

3 ounces feta cheese, crumbled

PER SERVING: Calories **348**; Protein **5g**; Carbohydrates **9g**; Dietary Fiber **3g**; Sugar **4g**; Total Fat **33g**; Saturated Fat **7g**

The Greeks have this simple salad of shredded romaine, dill, feta, and green onions lightly dressed with a lemon–olive oil dressing that I love. Like most Mediterranean dishes, maroulosalata is simple but full of flavor. While I like the crunch of romaine, it could use a little boost in the nutrient department, so I add shredded spinach, too. A bit of feta goes a long way—there's a big impact from just a small portion of the salty, creamy, briny cheese. A lovely light lunch as is, adding some grilled or pan-seared protein (see pages 48–49) will turn this delicious salad into a bona fide dinner.

1. In a small bowl, whisk together the lemon zest, lemon juice, and vinegar. Season with salt and pepper. Slowly whisk in the oil until emulsified.

2. In a large bowl, combine the lettuce, spinach, green onions, dill, and feta. Add the dressing, season with salt and pepper, and toss to combine. Let sit at room temperature for 5 minutes before serving.

Shaved Brussels Sprouts with Pomegranate-Orange Vinaigrette and Pecans

SERVES 4

2 navel oranges

Vinaigrette

3 tablespoons aged sherry vinegar

2 teaspoons pomegranate molasses

1 teaspoon finely grated orange zest

Kosher salt and freshly ground black pepper

¼ cup extra-virgin olive oil

Salad

1½ pounds Brussels sprouts, tough outer leaves removed, thinly sliced or shredded in a food processor

¼ cup pomegranate seeds

½ cup toasted pecans, chopped

PER SERVING: Calories **318**; Protein **7g**; Carbohydrates **20g**; Dietary Fiber **7g**; Sugar **7g**; Total Fat **24g**; Saturated Fat **3g**

I have been roasting Brussels sprouts at my restaurants for the past ten years and love the flavor and texture the intense heat brings to them. But now I have another favorite way to eat this member of the cruciferous vegetable: raw! They're wonderfully crunchy and slaw-like in a great way. No matter how you prep them, they're also surprisingly high in protein for a green vegetable, and just one serving meets your needs for vitamins C and K for the day.

1. Trim the top and bottom of each orange. Put the oranges on one flat end and remove the rest of the rind in strips. Working over a bowl (to catch the juice) slice just to the left and right of each membrane, freeing each perfect wedge. Slice each segment in half crosswise and set aside. Squeeze the rest of the juice from the empty membranes into the bowl.

2. Make the vinaigrette: To the bowl with the orange juice, add the vinegar, molasses, orange zest, and salt and pepper to taste, and whisk to combine. Slowly add the oil, whisking until emulsified.

3. Toss the salad: In a large bowl, combine the shaved sprouts, the reserved orange segments, and the pomegranate seeds, add the vinaigrette, and toss to combine. Let sit at room temperature for 30 minutes before serving or cover and refrigerate for up to 8 hours. Transfer to a platter and garnish with the pecans.

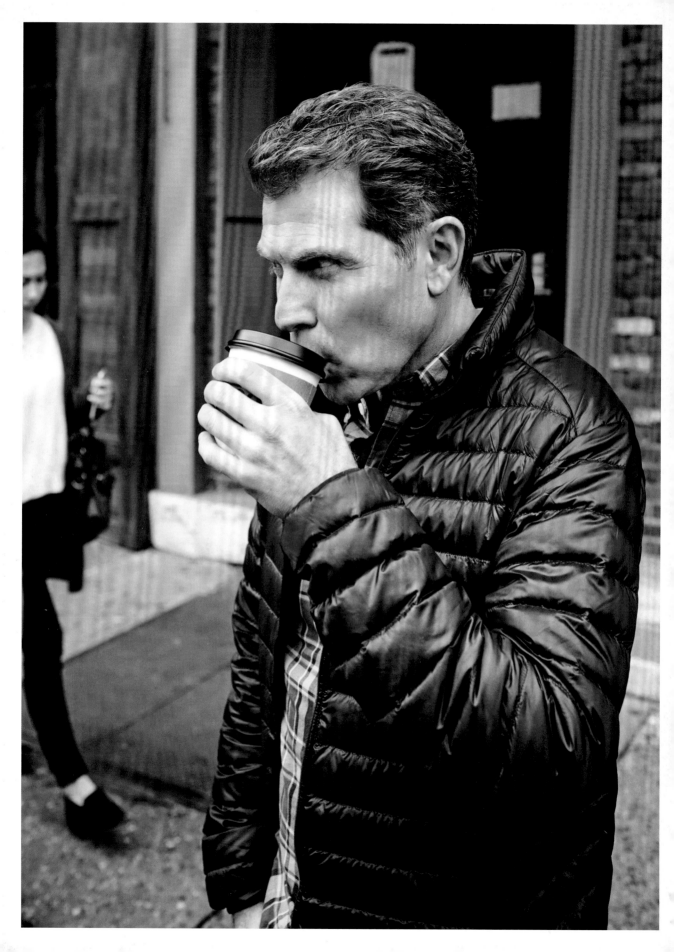

SOUPS

Best Vegetable Stock

MAKES 7 CUPS

8 ounces cremini mushrooms, halved

2 plum tomatoes, halved

6 celery stalks, cut into 2-inch pieces

1 medium Spanish onion, cut into 2-inch pieces

2 large carrots, peeled and cut into 2-inch pieces

1 small fennel bulb, cut into 2-inch pieces

2 tablespoons olive oil

Kosher salt and freshly ground black pepper

1 cup dry white wine

4 quarts cold water

1 teaspoon black peppercorns

8 fresh thyme sprigs

Small bunch of fresh flat-leaf parsley

2 fresh bay leaves or 1 large dried

PER CUP: Calories **22**; Protein **0g**; Carbohydrates **5g**; Dietary Fiber **0g**; Sugar **2g**; Total Fat **0g**; Saturated Fat **0g**

Okay, I may be reaching with the title, but, I have to say: It's really, really good! And that is something that I never thought I would say about a vegetable stock. As a chef, I have relied on chicken stocks, fish stocks, veal stocks, and beef stocks in my cooking over the years. But with more and more people eating a vegetable-centric diet and demanding vegetarian dishes at my restaurants, it was time to come up with a truly flavorful stock that could be the base of great vegetarian sauces and soups. Like most stocks, this freezes very well; so do yourself a favor when making it and double the recipe to keep some on hand.

1. Preheat the oven to 350°F.

2. In a large roasting pan, combine the mushrooms, tomatoes, and vegetables, add the oil, and season lightly with salt and pepper. Toss to coat evenly. Roast, turning a few times, until softened, about 45 minutes.

3. Transfer the vegetables to a large stockpot and set over high heat. Add the wine and cook until it has evaporated completely. Add the water, peppercorns, thyme, parsley, and bay leaves and bring to a boil. Reduce the heat to low and simmer for 1½ hours, skimming the surface of impurities as needed. Remove from the heat, cover, and let sit for 30 minutes.

4. Strain the stock through a fine-mesh strainer into a large bowl, pressing on the cooked vegetables to get as much liquid as possible. You should have about 8 cups of stock. Return to the stockpot and bring to a boil over high heat. Cook until reduced by 1 cup.

5. Let cool to room temperature, transfer to a container with a lid, and refrigerate for up to 4 days or freeze for up to 3 months.

Best Chicken Stock

MAKES 6 CUPS

1 (4-pound) whole chicken

2 medium carrots, peeled and cut into 1-inch pieces

2 medium celery stalks, cut into 2-inch pieces

1 medium yellow onion, skin left on, cut into ½-inch wedges

Small bunch of fresh flat-leaf parsley

6 fresh thyme sprigs

12 black peppercorns

1 tablespoon kosher salt

PER CUP: Calories **15**; Protein **2g**; Carbohydrates **2g**; Dietary Fiber **0g**; Sugar **0g**; Total Fat **0g**; Saturated Fat **0g**

When you start a dish with a homemade stock, you don't have to worry about BPA-lined cans or strange preservatives. It is easy to make, it freezes beautifully, and most important, homemade chicken stock simply has so much flavor. As a bonus, this recipe results in one fully cooked, moist, poached chicken, perfect for sandwiches and salads—or for dropping into soups before serving.

1. In a large pot or Dutch oven, combine the chicken, carrots, celery, onion, parsley, thyme, and peppercorns. Cover with cold water by 2 inches (should be 12 cups) and add the salt. Bring to a boil over high heat, reduce the heat to low, and simmer, partially covered, for 30 minutes.

2. Remove the chicken, let cool slightly, and then remove the meat from the bones. Discard the skin. Return the carcass to the pot and continue cooking, skimming impurities from the surface as needed, for 2 hours longer. Once the meat is cool, cover and refrigerate for up to 2 days.

3. Remove the carcass and discard. Strain the stock through a fine-mesh strainer into a clean pot, bring to a boil, and cook until reduced to 6 cups.

4. Let cool to room temperature, transfer to a container with a lid, and refrigerate for up to 4 days or freeze for up to 3 months.

Roasted Lemon Chicken Brodo

MAKES 8 CUPS

1 (4-pound) whole chicken, cut into 8 pieces, rinsed well and patted dry

8 chicken wings, rinsed well and patted dry

2 lemons, halved

1 large Spanish onion, skin left on, halved

2 medium carrots, peeled and coarsely chopped

2 medium celery stalks, coarsely chopped

2 tablespoons canola oil

Kosher salt and freshly ground black pepper

2 plum tomatoes, chopped

12 fresh flat-leaf parsley sprigs

8 fresh thyme sprigs

1 bay leaf

12 black peppercorns

2 quarts Best Chicken Stock (page 141) or low-sodium store-bought

1 teaspoon finely grated lemon zest

PER CUP: Calories **30**; Protein **4g**; Carbohydrates **4g**; Dietary Fiber **0g**; Sugar **0g**; Total Fat **0g**; Saturated Fat **0g**

Brodo, the Italian word for bone broth, is a super-enriched stock that became popular in New York City a few years ago when a talented chef named Marco Canora opened up a little broth bar in the East Village. His incredibly rich, delicious broth is made from roasted beef bones simmered for hours and hours in chicken stock—what's often called a "double" stock—and people are crazy for its nutrient-packed, soothing powers. Chicken is lighter than beef, of course, yet roasting its bones also creates great depth of flavor and richness. Roasted lemon adds a fantastic touch of sweet, bright acidity. This is my "green juice," what I get when I need a pick-me-up, but please don't save it for a sick day—it also works wonderfully as a hearty chicken stock in sauces and gravies.

1. Preheat the oven to 425°F.

2. On a large rimmed baking sheet, toss the chicken pieces, lemons, onion, carrots, and celery with the oil and season lightly with salt and pepper. Spread the ingredients in a single layer and roast, turning the chicken and vegetables over once halfway through, until golden brown, 30 to 40 minutes.

3. Remove the lemons, let cool slightly, and then squeeze their juice into a measuring cup. Cover and refrigerate until needed.

4. Transfer the remaining mixture to a large stockpot, add the tomatoes, parsley, thyme, bay leaf, peppercorns, 2 teaspoons salt, the stock, and 1 quart water, and bring to a boil over high heat. Reduce the heat to low, partially cover, and simmer the stock for 3 hours.

5. Strain the mixture through a strainer into a clean large saucepan, set over high heat, and reduce until you have about 8 cups remaining, about 40 minutes.

6. Add the reserved lemon juice and the grated zest and season with salt and pepper. Serve hot in mugs.

Red Curry Cauliflower Soup with Cauliflower "Croutons"

SERVES 6

3 tablespoons coconut oil or olive oil

1 medium sweet onion, such as Vidalia, coarsely chopped

2 tablespoons plus 2 teaspoons Thai red curry paste

½ cup dry white wine, such as Pinot Grigio

2 cups Best Vegetable Stock (page 140) or low-sodium store-bought

1 large head of cauliflower, broken into small florets

1 (14-ounce) can light coconut milk

½ teaspoon sugar

Kosher salt and freshly ground black pepper

¼ cup chopped green onions, dark and pale green parts

Lime wedges, for serving

PER SERVING: Calories **165**; Protein **3g**; Carbohydrates **13g**; Dietary Fiber **4g**; Sugar **7g**; Total Fat **11g**; Saturated Fat **9g**

Don't let the red color fool you; this soup definitely has a kick, but it's not burn-your-mouth hot. Thai red curry paste is a combination of red chiles, coriander roots and leaves, shrimp paste, lemongrass, garlic, shallots, and galangal. It's spicy, sweet, salty, and altogether distinctively delicious. I use it in soups, sauces, and, of course, curries. Red curry paste—or any curry paste for that matter—is a great way to adds loads of flavor without unwanted fat and calories. Keep things on the light side and opt for low-fat coconut milk, still lush, creamy, and oh-so coconutty.

1. Preheat the oven to 375°F.

2. In a medium Dutch oven, heat 2 tablespoons of the oil over medium heat until it shimmers. Add the onion and cook until soft, about 4 minutes. Add 2 tablespoons of the curry paste and cook, stirring constantly, for 2 minutes. Add the wine and cook until reduced by half.

3. Add the stock and bring to a simmer. Reserve 1 cup of the cauliflower florets and add the remaining cauliflower to the pan. Simmer for 10 minutes. Add the coconut milk and sugar, season with salt and pepper, and cook until the cauliflower is very soft, about 10 minutes longer. Remove from the heat and let cool slightly.

4. While the soup is cooking, in a small bowl whisk together the remaining 1 tablespoon oil and the remaining 2 teaspoons curry paste and season with salt and pepper. Add the reserved cauliflower florets, toss to coat, and spread on a rimmed baking sheet in an even layer. Roast until golden brown and crispy, turning once, about 20 minutes.

5. In batches, if necessary, transfer the cauliflower soup to a blender and blend until smooth. Return the soup to the pot and simmer over medium heat until slightly thickened, about 10 minutes longer.

6. Ladle the soup into bowls, top with a few of the golden cauliflower "croutons," and garnish with green onion. Squeeze lime juice on top.

Vegetarian Chili with Roasted Sweet Potatoes and Pepper Vinegar

SERVES 6

2 sweet potatoes (1 pound), peeled and cut into ½-inch dice

4 tablespoons olive oil

Kosher salt and ground black pepper

1 medium red onion, finely diced

1 large poblano chile, seeded and finely diced

1 yellow bell pepper, seeded, and finely diced

3 garlic cloves, finely chopped

1 tablespoon pure chile powder (such as ancho)

2 teaspoons ground cumin

1 teaspoon ground coriander

¼ teaspoon ground cayenne pepper

2 teaspoons dried oregano, preferably Mexican

2 cups Best Vegetable Stock (page 140) or low-sodium store-bought

1 (28-ounce) can plum tomatoes and juices, coarsely pureed or crushed

1 (15.5-ounce) can black beans, drained, rinsed, and drained again

1 (15.5-ounce) can chickpeas, drained, rinsed, and drained again

¼ cup chopped fresh cilantro

3 green onions, dark and pale green parts, thinly sliced

Pepper Vinegar (recipe follows)

12 Baked Collard Chips (page 98)

PER SERVING: Calories **334**; Protein **11g**; Carbohydrates **47g**; Dietary Fiber **13g**; Sugar **12g**; Total Fat **12g**; Saturated Fat **2g**

So much more than a vegetable stew, this dish attains its authentically deep chili flavor from the combination of fresh chiles and dried spices, as well as the usual savory suspects, onion and garlic. About those spices: This isn't the time to skip a step and try a prepackaged "chili powder" blend; you'll get a much deeper, more complex flavor if you make the effort to find and combine the individual spices, from smoky cumin to fiery cayenne. A dash of pepper vinegar adds just the right touch of acidity when serving, and every chili is made better by a little crunch. Try salty Baked Collard Chips (page 98) for a healthy, delicious option.

1. Preheat the oven to 400°F.

2. On a rimmed baking sheet, toss the sweet potatoes with 2 tablespoons of the oil and season with salt and pepper. Spread the sweet potatoes in an even layer and roast, turning once, until soft and lightly golden brown, about 25 minutes.

3. While the sweet potatoes are roasting, heat the remaining 2 tablespoons oil in a large saucepan over medium-high heat until it begins to shimmer. Add the onion, poblano, and bell pepper and cook until soft, about 5 minutes. Add the garlic and cook for 1 minute. Add the chile powder, cumin, coriander, cayenne, and oregano and cook for 2 minutes.

4. Add the stock and tomatoes and bring to a boil, season with salt and pepper, and cook, stirring occasionally, until reduced and slightly thickened, about 30 minutes. Add the black beans and chickpeas and cook for 15 minutes longer. Add the sweet potatoes and cook until just heated through, about 5 minutes. Check for seasoning and stir in the cilantro and green onions.

5. Ladle the chili into bowls, add a few dashes of pepper vinegar, and top each with a couple of collard chips.

Pepper Vinegar

MAKES 1 CUP

1 cup red wine vinegar

1 fresno or jalapeño pepper, thinly sliced

Combine the vinegar and pepper in a small bowl and let sit at room temperature for at least 1 hour or cover and refrigerate for up to 2 days.

PER TABLESPOON: Calories **0**; Protein **0g**; Carbohydrates **0g**; Dietary Fiber **0g**; Sugar **0g**; Total Fat **0g**; Saturated Fat **0g**

Mushroom Barley Soup

SERVES 4

2 pounds assorted mushrooms (cremini, shiitake, white), stems removed and reserved, caps coarsely chopped

2 tablespoons olive oil

2 teaspoons chopped fresh thyme

Kosher salt and freshly ground black pepper

4 cups Best Vegetable Stock (page 140) or low-sodium store-bought

½ cup hulled barley

2 carrots, peeled and cut into ½-inch dice

2 tablespoons chopped fresh flat-leaf parsley

Squeeze of fresh lemon juice

PER SERVING: Calories **227**; Protein **7g**; Carbohydrates **33g**; Dietary Fiber **2g**; Sugar **11g**; Total Fat **8g**; Saturated Fat **1g**

This warm, hearty soup is proof positive that not all comfort foods need be guilt-inducing. Mushrooms are low in calories, fat-free, cholesterol-free, gluten-free, and very low in sodium, yet they provide important nutrients, including selenium, potassium, riboflavin, niacin, and vitamin D. Also, they have a very meaty taste and texture that vegetarians and carnivores alike love. I like roasting them in a hot oven to intensify the flavor. Hulled barley is a wonderfully versatile grain with a rich nutlike flavor and an appealing chewy, pasta-like consistency. If you can't find hulled barley, pearl barley works nicely, too, and takes half the time to cook.

1. Preheat the oven to 400°F.

2. Put the mushroom caps on a rimmed baking sheet, drizzle with the oil, and season with the thyme and some salt and pepper. Mix to combine and then spread out in an even layer. Roast, stirring a few times, until golden brown and the mushrooms' liquid has evaporated, about 40 minutes.

3. While the mushrooms are roasting, in a medium pot combine the stock, 2 cups water, and the mushroom stems and bring to a boil over high heat. Reduce the heat so that the liquid simmers and cook for 20 minutes. Remove from the heat, cover, and let steep for another 20 minutes. Strain the stock into a medium stockpot, discarding the stems.

4. Add the barley and simmer over medium heat for 20 minutes. Add the roasted mushrooms and the carrots and continue cooking until the barley is tender, about 20 minutes longer. Season with salt and pepper and stir in the parsley and a squeeze of lemon juice.

"Grilled Cheese" and Tomato Soup

SERVES 4

2 pounds ripe tomatoes (any kind), cored and halved if large

1 small sweet onion, such as Vidalia or Walla Walla, coarsely chopped

2 tablespoons olive oil

Kosher salt and freshly ground black pepper

1 cup dry white wine

¼ cup fresh cilantro, flat-leaf parsley, or basil, plus more for serving

4 Frico (page 42), made with Gruyère cheese

PER SERVING: Calories **236**; Protein **9g**; Carbohydrates **13g**; Dietary Fiber **3g**; Sugar **7g**; Total Fat **17g**; Saturated Fat **6g**

This soup is so easy and healthy. Even better: it's delicious. My tomato soup tastes like tomato—not garlic or a wild blend of herbs or tons of spices. Get your hands on great tomatoes and keep it simple. Though I do love dipping a buttery grilled cheese sandwich in this soup, I've found another way to have my cheese and eat it, too: the frico—no butter, no bread, just a small crisp circle of cheese to dip and melt into all sorts of tasty goodness.

1. Preheat the oven to 300°F.

2. On a rimmed baking sheet, combine the tomatoes and onion, add the oil, and season with salt and pepper. Toss to coat. Roast until the tomatoes and onion are soft, but not colored, about an hour.

3. Transfer the mixture to a medium saucepan, add the wine, and cook over high heat until the wine has evaporated. Add enough cold water just to cover the tops of the tomatoes, season with salt and pepper, and simmer, stirring occasionally, until the mixture begins to thicken, about 20 minutes.

4. Transfer the mixture to a blender, add the herbs, and carefully blend until smooth. Return the soup to the pot and boil over high heat for 5 minutes longer to thicken slightly.

5. Ladle the soup into bowls, top each bowl with a frico and additional chopped herbs, and serve.

VARIATION

Cream of Tomato Soup

For a creamy but still sensible version, take the pot off the heat and, before serving, stir in 2 tablespoons 2% Greek yogurt and 2 tablespoons half-and-half. Calories **139**; Protein **3g**; Sugar **8g**; Total Fat **9g**; Saturated Fat **2g**

Salsa Verde Chicken Soup with Roasted Hominy

SERVES 6

1 (15.5-ounce) can posole, drained, rinsed, and drained again

2 tablespoons olive oil

1 tablespoon dried oregano, preferably Mexican

Kosher salt and freshly ground black pepper

4 cups Best Chicken Stock (page 141) or low-sodium store-bought

1 pound boneless, skinless chicken thighs

Salsa Verde (recipe follows)

¼ cup chopped fresh cilantro

PER SERVING (INCLUDES SALSA): Calories **296**; Protein **21g**; Carbohydrates **13g**; Dietary Fiber **2g**; Sugar **2g**; Total Fat **17g**; Saturated Fat **3g**

For those unfamiliar with the Mexican standards, this is a riff on one of my favorites, posole, which is basically a meat-and-hominy-laden, chile-scented chicken soup. It's so comforting, so flavorful, and so nourishing that, if I were a doctor, I'd prescribe a big bowl of this to every cold-ridden patient who came to my door. Roasting the posole in the oven (it turns golden and crisp, almost like a baked corn nut!) and adding it to the soup like a garnish creates a dynamic new texture play as well as another layer of toasty flavor. Salsa verde—a green Mexican sauce of roasted tomatillos, onions, garlic, and chiles combined with tart lime juice and herbaceous cilantro—instantly brightens the soup.

1. Preheat the oven to 400°F.

2. Put the posole on paper towels to dry. Transfer to a rimmed baking sheet and toss with the oil, oregano, and salt and pepper to taste. Bake until lightly golden brown and crispy, turning every 10 minutes, about 35 minutes.

3. In a medium stockpot, bring the chicken stock and 2 cups water to a simmer, add the chicken, and simmer for 5 minutes. Turn off the heat and let the chicken sit in the hot broth for 5 minutes longer until cooked through. Remove the chicken to a plate, let cool slightly, and then shred into bite-size pieces.

4. Return the liquid to a simmer, add the salsa verde, and cook for 5 minutes. Return the chicken to the pot and cook for 5 minutes longer to heat through.

5. Ladle the soup into bowls, add the roasted posole, and garnish with the cilantro.

Salsa Verde

MAKES ABOUT 1 CUP

6 medium tomatillos, husked and scrubbed

1 small red onion, coarsely chopped

2 garlic cloves, smashed

2 jalapeño peppers, coarsely chopped

2 tablespoons olive oil

Kosher salt and freshly ground black pepper

Juice of 2 limes

¼ cup chopped fresh cilantro

1. Preheat the oven to 375°F.

2. On a rimmed baking sheet, toss the tomatillos, onion, garlic, and jalapeños in the oil and season with salt and black pepper. Spread in a single layer and roast, stirring once, until the vegetables are golden brown and soft, about 30 minutes.

3. Transfer the mixture to a food processor, add the lime juice and cilantro, and process until smooth. Once cool, the salsa verde can be covered and refrigerated for up to 2 days.

PER 2 TABLESPOONS:
Calories **48**; Protein **0g**; Carbohydrates **4g**; Dietary Fiber **1g**; Sugar **1g**; Total Fat **4g**; Saturated Fat **1g**

Moroccan Lamb Chili with Toasted Almond Couscous

SERVES 8

4 tablespoons olive oil

2 pounds lamb shoulder, trimmed of all fat, cut into ½-inch dice

Kosher salt and freshly ground black pepper

1 large Spanish onion, diced

1 large carrot, peeled and diced

1 red bell pepper, seeded and finely diced

3 garlic cloves, finely chopped

1 tablespoon smoked paprika

2 teaspoons ground cumin

2 teaspoons ground coriander

1 teaspoon ground allspice

2 tablespoons harissa paste

½ cup dry red wine (optional)

1 (28-ounce) can plum tomatoes and juices, coarsely pureed or crushed

2 cups Best Chicken Stock (page 141) or low-sodium store-bought

8 leaves of mustard greens or collard greens, coarsely chopped

2 (15.5-ounce) cans chickpeas, drained, rinsed, and drained again

¼ cup chopped fresh cilantro

Toasted Almond Couscous (recipe follows)

PER SERVING (INCLUDES COUSCOUS): Calories **419**; Protein **30g**; Carbohydrates **36g**; Dietary Fiber **12g**; Sugar **6g**; Total Fat **18g**; Saturated Fat **4g**

There is nothing more satisfying on a cold winter's day than a bowl of chili; just add a close game of football on TV, and I'm in heaven. This hearty version is full of vegetables and protein, with chickpeas and lamb in the starring roles. Where you can get in trouble with chili is with the garnishes—like when all that cheese, guacamole, sour cream, and those fried tortilla chips take up more room in the bowl than the chili! In part to keep the Tex-Mex temptations at bay and in part because I love the flavors, I opt for a Moroccan-inspired version served over whole-wheat couscous spiked with almonds and cilantro. If lamb is not your thing, lean ground beef works perfectly in its place.

1. In a medium Dutch oven, heat 2 tablespoons of the oil over high heat until it shimmers. Working in batches if needed, add the lamb, season with salt and black pepper, and cook until golden brown, 8 minutes. Remove with a slotted spoon to a plate lined with paper towels. Once all of the lamb has been browned, drain any fat from the pot and wipe out the pot with a paper towel.

2. Heat the remaining 2 tablespoons oil in the pot over medium heat until it shimmers. Add the onion, carrot, and bell pepper and cook until soft. Add the garlic and cook for 1 minute. Stir in the paprika, cumin, coriander, allspice, and harissa and cook, stirring constantly, for 2 minutes. Add the wine, if using, and cook until it has evaporated.

3. Add the tomatoes and chicken stock and bring to a simmer. Return the lamb to the pot and bring to a boil. Reduce the heat to low, cover, and cook until the lamb is tender, about 1½ hours.

4. Remove the lamb to a plate with a slotted spoon, bring the cooking liquid to a boil, and cook until reduced slightly, about 15 minutes.

5. Return the lamb to the pot, add the mustard greens and chickpeas, and simmer for 10 minutes. Season with salt and black pepper and stir in the cilantro. Serve the chili in bowls over the couscous.

Toasted Almond Couscous

SERVES 8

Kosher salt and freshly ground
    black pepper

2 cups whole-wheat couscous

½ cup lightly toasted slivered
    almonds

¼ cup chopped fresh cilantro

1. In a medium saucepan, bring 2 cups water to a boil, season with salt and pepper, and add the couscous. Remove from the heat, cover, and let sit until the water is absorbed, about 5 minutes.

2. Remove the lid, fluff the couscous with a fork, and stir in the almonds and cilantro.

PER SERVING: Calories **267**; Protein **10g**; Carbohydrates **47g**; Dietary Fiber **8g**; Sugar **0g**; Total Fat **5g**; Saturated Fat **0g**

DINNER

Veggie Burger

SERVES 4

Burgers

1 (15.5-ounce) cans chickpeas, drained, rinsed, and drained again on paper towels for at least 15 minutes

Kosher salt and freshly ground black pepper

1 cup (loosely packed) quinoa

2 tablespoons canola oil, plus ½ cup for frying

1 pound cremini mushrooms, stemmed and sliced about ¼ inch thick

Scant ¼ cup barbecue sauce

¼ cup chopped fresh cilantro

2 large eggs

1½ cups quinoa flour

Sauce

3 tablespoons Dijon mustard

3 tablespoons whole-grain mustard

1 tablespoon red wine vinegar

1 teaspoon honey

¼ cup sliced green onion, dark and pale green parts

Kosher salt and freshly ground black pepper

PER SERVING: Calories **555**; Protein **23g**; Carbohydrates **79g**; Dietary Fiber **13g**; Sugar **6g**; Total Fat **17g**; Saturated Fat **2g**

Full disclosure: I had never met a veggie burger that I liked—until now, that is. A few months ago, I had to create a veggie burger on the fly for a battle on my show *Beat Bobby Flay*. Don't ask me what made me grab mushrooms, quinoa, and chickpeas off the pantry shelves, but I am glad I did. The trio makes a perfect combination of flavors and textures. The star ingredient is the quinoa flour, found just about everywhere these days; it provides crunch that regular all-purpose flour doesn't. While this burger is not a hamburger, I still think it is pretty delicious, and it's now featured at all the Bobby's Burger Palaces. Top it as you like and serve it on your favorite bun.

1. Make the burgers: Line a rimmed baking sheet with absorbent kitchen towels or paper towels. In a food processor, coarsely puree the drained chickpeas. You need ½ cup.

2. In a medium saucepan, combine 2 cups water and 2 teaspoons salt and bring to a boil over high heat. Stir in the quinoa and return to a boil. Reduce the heat to low, cover, and simmer until the quinoa is tender and the water has been absorbed, about 25 minutes. Remove from the heat, let sit for 10 minutes, and then fluff with a fork. Spread the quinoa evenly onto the prepared baking sheet and let cool completely. The quinoa can be cooked a day ahead and stored in a container with a tight-fitting lid in the refrigerator.

3. In a large sauté pan, heat the 2 tablespoons oil over high heat until the oil begins to shimmer. Add the mushrooms and cook for 3 minutes without touching. Stir and then cook until the mushrooms are golden brown and dry, 10 minutes.

4. Add the barbecue sauce and a splash of water to the mushrooms and cook until the mushrooms are glazed, about 2 minutes; transfer to a medium bowl and let cool to room temperature.

5. Mix the quinoa, chickpea puree, and cilantro into the mushrooms and season with salt and pepper if needed. Cover the mixture and refrigerate until chilled, at least 2 hours.

(Recipe continues)

6. Make the sauce: In a small bowl, whisk together the mustards, vinegar, honey, and salt and pepper to taste. Set aside.

7. In a shallow bowl, whisk together the eggs and a tablespoon of water and season with ¼ teaspoon salt and ⅛ teaspoon pepper. Put the quinoa flour on a small plate and whisk in 1 teaspoon salt and ⅛ teaspoon pepper.

8. Form the mushroom mixture into 4 burgers (I like to use a 4-inch ring mold). Set a burger on a slotted metal spatula and gently dip it into the egg bath. Remove and let excess drip off. Dredge in the quinoa flour and tap off the excess. Transfer to a plate. Repeat with the remaining 3 burgers.

9. In a large nonstick sauté pan, heat ½ cup oil over high heat until it begins to simmer. Fry the burgers in the hot oil until golden brown and crisp, about 2 minutes per side. Drain on a plate lined with paper towels before serving with the mustard–green onion sauce.

Stuffed Poblano Chiles with Israeli Couscous Ratatouille

SERVES 4

4 poblano chiles

1 tablespoon canola oil

Kosher salt and freshly ground black pepper

1 small zucchini, diced

1 small yellow squash, diced

1 Japanese eggplant, diced

1 cup grape tomatoes, halved

1 cup canned chickpeas, drained, rinsed, and drained again

1 small red onion, halved and thinly sliced

2 garlic cloves, coarsely chopped

2 tablespoons olive oil

1½ cups Best Vegetable Stock (page 140) or low-sodium store-bought

1 cup whole-wheat Israeli couscous

2 tablespoons chopped fresh basil

2 tablespoons chopped fresh flat-leaf parsley

2 ounces soft goat cheese, crumbled

½ recipe Roasted Red Pepper Tomato Sauce (page 29), hot

PER SERVING: Calories **518**; Protein **16g**; Carbohydrates **72g**; Dietary Fiber **13g**; Sugar **3g**; Total Fat **19g**; Saturated Fat **4g**

Chiles rellenos, or stuffed chiles, have been appearing on my menus since my days at Miracle Grill, which was practically a lifetime ago, and I see no reason to stop now. Peppery, though generally not "hot" (keep in mind that each one has a mind and heat scale of its own, however!), green poblanos are my favorite for stuffing, and I've found them to be a fantastic way to usher vegetarian dishes to the table. This filling—a quick-roasted ratatouille of garlicky eggplant, summer squashes, tomatoes, and red onion—is more Provençal in provenance than American Southwestern, but it works all the same. While I love the creamy tang of goat cheese crumbled and folded in with the filling, you could easily leave it out to make this a vegan-friendly dish.

1. Preheat the oven to 400°F.

2. Rub the poblano chiles with the canola oil and season with salt and pepper. Roast on a rimmed baking sheet until soft and the skin is blackened, about 20 minutes. Transfer to a bowl (keep the oven on), cover with plastic wrap, and let steam for 10 minutes. Remove and discard the skin from each chile. Make a slit down the center of each chile and carefully, trying not to tear the chile, remove the seeds.

3. On a rimmed baking sheet, toss the zucchini, yellow squash, eggplant, tomatoes, chickpeas, onion, and garlic with the olive oil and season with salt and pepper. Spread in an even layer and roast, turning once, until soft and golden brown, about 25 minutes.

4. In a small saucepan, bring the stock to a boil over high heat. Add 1 teaspoon salt and ¼ teaspoon pepper, stir in the couscous, and cook until tender and the water is absorbed, about 12 minutes.

5. Drain off any excess water if need be and transfer the couscous to a bowl. Stir in the roasted vegetables, basil, parsley, and cheese and season with salt and pepper.

6. Carefully fill each poblano chile with the vegetable mixture. Ladle some of the sauce into large shallow bowls or dinner plates and top with the poblanos.

Eggplant Parmesan Redux

SERVES 6

Bread Crumbs

2 tablespoons olive oil

1½ cups panko bread crumbs

2 tablespoons freshly grated
  Parmigiano-Reggiano cheese

Finely grated zest of 1 lemon

Kosher salt and freshly ground black
  pepper

Eggplant

2 medium eggplants, sliced
  lengthwise into ¼-inch-thick slices

¼ cup olive oil

Kosher salt and freshly ground black
  pepper

2 cups Roasted Red Pepper Tomato
  Sauce (page 29)

¼ cup freshly grated Parmigiano-
  Reggiano cheese

Fresh basil, for garnish

PER SERVING: Calories **279**;
Protein **6g**; Carbohydrates **24g**;
Dietary Fiber **6g**; Sugar **8g**; Total Fat
18g; Saturated Fat **3g**

In Italy, eggplant Parmesan is actually a rather healthy dish of eggplant sautéed in olive oil and then layered in a simple tomato sauce with fresh herbs and a sprinkling of Parmesan cheese. We Americans were the ones to coat that eggplant in breading, deep-fry it, and weight it down even further with pools of mozzarella. I've titled this recipe Eggplant Parmesan Redux, but actually, this is the way it was meant to be.

1. Make the bread crumbs: In a large nonstick pan, heat the oil over medium heat until it begins to shimmer. Add the bread crumbs and cook, stirring constantly, until pale golden brown, about 4 minutes. Remove to a bowl and stir in the cheese, lemon zest, and salt and pepper to taste.

2. Roast the eggplant: Preheat the oven to 425°F.

3. Line 2 rimmed baking sheets with parchment paper and divide the eggplant between the 2 pans in a single layer. Brush both sides with the oil and season with salt and pepper. Bake, turning once, until golden brown on both sides and tender, about 30 minutes. Remove from the oven.

4. Reduce the oven temperature to 375°F.

5. Spread ¼ cup of the sauce into a 9-inch square baking dish. Add a layer of eggplant, another ¼ cup of the sauce, more eggplant, and a little of the cheese, and repeat until all of the ingredients have been used.

6. Put the baking dish on a rimmed baking sheet and bake until the sauce begins to bubble, about 30 minutes. Sprinkle the bread crumbs evenly over the top, return to the oven, and bake until the crumbs are golden brown, 10 minutes longer.

7. Remove from the oven and let rest for 10 minutes before serving. Garnish with basil.

Steamed Halibut in Saffron-Tomato Broth

SERVES 4

2 tablespoons olive oil

2 shallots, halved and thinly sliced

1 garlic clove, thinly sliced

5 anchovy fillets, chopped

Pinch of red pepper flakes, preferably Calabrian

½ cup white wine

1 (28-ounce) can plum tomatoes and their juices, pureed until smooth

1 cup clam juice or fish stock

Large pinch of saffron threads

4 (5-ounce) skinless halibut fillets

Kosher salt and freshly ground black pepper

½ cup thinly sliced black or green brined olives

2 tablespoons chopped fresh mint

½ cup Crispy Whole-Wheat Couscous (page 39)

PER SERVING: Calories **384**; Protein **35g**; Carbohydrates **24g**; Dietary Fiber **6g**; Sugar **7g**; Total Fat **16g**; Saturated Fat **2g**

Saffron-scented anything, when handled with a deft touch, tastes luxurious. I'm not sure if it's because I know how much those precious tins cost and how long it takes to fill each one, but I do know that I feel like I'm treating myself to something good when I taste it. This dish of lean, flaky white fish steamed with the barest touch of oil is as healthy as they come, and yet it tastes so good and that orangey-red broth is so enticing, that it feels practically indulgent. Punctuated with salty sliced olives and herbaceous fresh mint, this might be the healthiest, tastiest way to treat yourself that you've come upon in ages.

1. In a medium sauté pan with high sides, heat the oil over medium heat until it begins to shimmer. Add the shallots and garlic and cook for 1 minute. Add the anchovies and cook until they melt into the oil, another minute. Add the red pepper flakes and cook for 30 seconds longer.

2. Add the wine and simmer until it has reduced by half. Add the tomato puree, clam juice, and saffron, bring to a boil, and cook until slightly thickened, about 25 minutes.

3. Season the halibut on both sides with salt and black pepper and add to the pan. Reduce the heat to low, cover the pan, and cook until the fish is just cooked through, about 10 minutes. Remove the fish to a plate and loosely cover with foil to keep warm.

4. Return the sauce to high heat and boil until slightly thickened, about 10 minutes. Season lightly with salt and pepper and then stir in the olives and mint. Ladle some of the sauce into the bottom of each bowl, top with halibut, and spoon some of the olives over the top and garnish with crispy couscous.

Seared Sea Bass with Green Gazpacho Relish

SERVES 4

¼ cup extra-virgin olive oil

Finely grated zest of 1 lime

Juice of 2 limes

1 teaspoon clover honey

1 garlic clove, smashed to a paste

1 serrano pepper, finely diced

Kosher salt and freshly ground black pepper

1 ripe Hass avocado, peeled, pitted, and finely diced

½ English cucumber, finely diced

1 large green zebra heirloom tomato, diced, or 8 green zebra cherry tomatoes, quartered

1 large green onion, dark and pale green parts, thinly sliced

2 tablespoons finely chopped fresh cilantro, plus whole leaves for garnish

2 tablespoons olive oil

4 (6-ounce) skinless sea bass fillets

PER SERVING: Calories **443**; Protein **33g**; Carbohydrates **10g**; Dietary Fiber **2g**; Sugar **4g**; Total Fat **31g**; Saturated Fat **5g**

I can't think of a dish better suited to a summer evening: so fresh, green, and flavorful. All of the best parts of a cool tomato gazpacho—juicy tomato, pungent onion, spicy chiles, refreshing cucumber—are diced, mixed with creamy avocado and verdant cilantro, and showered in fresh lime juice. Using slightly tart green zebra tomatoes makes this dish a total monochromatic stunner, but you could use red tomatoes for a version that's just as tasty.

1. In a large bowl, whisk together the ¼ cup extra-virgin olive oil, lime zest and juice, honey, garlic, serrano, 1 teaspoon salt, and ⅛ teaspoon black pepper in a large bowl and let sit for 10 minutes. Add the avocado, cucumber, tomato, green onion, and chopped cilantro and stir until combined. Cover and let sit at room temperature for at least 15 minutes and up to 1 hour before serving.

2. In a large nonstick sauté pan, heat the 2 tablespoons olive oil over high heat until it begins to shimmer. Season the bass on both sides with salt and black pepper.

3. Cook the fish until lightly golden brown on both sides and just cooked through, about 4 minutes per side. Serve in shallow bowls topped with large spoonfuls of the gazpacho relish. Garnish with cilantro leaves.

Spiced Salmon with Shaved Beet, Fennel, Lemon, and Herbs

SERVES 8

1 (3-pound) skinless center-cut piece of salmon fillet, pin bones removed

2 tablespoons olive oil

Kosher salt and freshly ground black pepper

¼ cup spice rub, homemade (see pages 35–37) or store-bought

1 large beet, peeled, halved, and sliced paper thin

1 large fennel bulb, cut in quarters and sliced paper thin

½ cup chopped assorted fresh herbs (flat-leaf parsley, tarragon, chives, dill, and/or cilantro)

¼ cup fresh lemon juice

¼ cup extra-virgin olive oil

¼ cup Spiced Almonds (page 43), chopped

PER SERVING: Calories **384**; Protein **35g**; Carbohydrates **5g**; Dietary Fiber **2g**; Sugar **2g**; Total Fat **24g**; Saturated Fat **3g**

There are few things as impressive as a perfectly cooked center-cut piece of salmon on a platter, whether smoked and presented with bagels and cream cheese for breakfast, or poached and paired with homemade mayonnaise for a buffet, or—my favorite way—simply roasted and served with thinly sliced raw beets and fennel and dressed with a lemon vinaigrette. This is an ideal dish for a weekend brunch, a ladies-who-lunch luncheon, or a light dinner. So easy, so elegant, and so healthy!

1. Remove the salmon from the refrigerator 1 hour before baking to ensure even cooking.

2. Preheat the oven to 375°F.

3. Put the salmon in a large baking dish or on a rimmed baking sheet. Brush the surface with the 2 tablespoons olive oil, season with salt and pepper, and then sprinkle the spice rub over the surface of the salmon. Roast until the fish is just cooked through, 15 to 20 minutes. Remove from the oven and let rest for 5 minutes.

4. In a large bowl, combine the beet, fennel, herbs, lemon juice, and the ¼ cup extra-virgin olive oil. Season with salt and pepper and toss to mix.

5. If not serving the salmon in its baking vessel, use two large spatulas to carefully transfer it to a large serving platter. Pile the shaved vegetable salad across the top of the fish and top with the spiced almonds.

Slow-Roasted Cod with Avocado Salsa Verde and Pomegranate

SERVES 4

Cod is relatively inexpensive, easily found in fish markets, low in calories, and simple to cook. On its own it can be rather mild, but here the salsa of rich creamy avocado mixed with tart tomatillo and sweet pomegranates creates an explosion of flavors and textures in your mouth. This dish is as tasty as it is beautiful.

2 cups Salsa Verda (page 151) or 1 (16-ounce) jar salsa verde, preferably Frontera brand

1 ripe Hass avocado, peeled, pitted, and diced

Juice of 1 lime, plus lime wedges for serving

¼ cup fresh cilantro, plus more for garnish

Kosher salt and freshly ground black pepper

1½ pounds black cod fillet, skin on

2 tablespoons canola oil

¼ cup pomegranate seeds

PER SERVING: Calories **466**; Protein **21g**; Carbohydrates **15g**; Dietary Fiber **2g**; Sugar **6g**; Total Fat **36g**; Saturated Fat **6g**

1. Preheat the oven to 425°F.

2. Pour the salsa verde into a blender, add the avocado, lime juice, and a splash of water, and blend until smooth. Add the cilantro and pulse a few times to incorporate but make sure to leave some green flecks. Season with salt and pepper.

3. Brush the cod on both sides with the oil, season with salt and pepper, and put in a baking dish. Roast until just cooked through, about 30 minutes.

4. Top the cod with the avocado salsa verde and scatter the pomegranate seeds and cilantro leaves over the top. Serve hot or at room temperature with lime juice squeezed over it.

Slow-Cooked Arctic Char with Broccolini, Capers, and Serrano Pepper

SERVES 4

4 tablespoons olive oil

1 garlic clove, thinly sliced

1 pound broccolini, coarsely chopped

Kosher salt and freshly ground black pepper

1 serrano pepper, thinly sliced

¼ cup rice wine vinegar

2 tablespoons extra-virgin olive oil

2 tablespoons small capers, drained

1 pound 4 ounces skin-on arctic char or salmon fillet

PER SERVING: Calories **516**; Protein **31g**; Carbohydrates **8g**; Dietary Fiber **2g**; Sugar **3g**; Total Fat **39g**; Saturated Fat **7g**

I love Arctic char! Yes, it can be expensive and somewhat hard to find, but it is worth it. Slow roasting the fish in its own healthy fat gives it a buttery texture without using any butter. Contrary to popular belief, broccolini is not baby broccoli; it's actually a cross between regular broccoli and Chinese broccoli. The capers and serrano offer a bit of acidity and heat to counter the rich-tasting fish. Arctic char is closely related to salmon and trout—so, if you can't find it in your local fish store, feel free to substitute either one.

1. Preheat the oven to 400°F.

2. In a small saucepan or skillet, heat 2 tablespoons of the olive oil over low heat, add the garlic, and cook until soft, about 2 minutes. Let sit for 5 minutes and then scoop out and discard the garlic.

3. Toss the broccolini with the garlic oil on a rimmed baking sheet and season with salt and black pepper. Roast until golden brown and crisp-tender, about 15 minutes.

4. While the broccolini is roasting, combine the serrano and vinegar in a small bowl and let sit for 15 minutes. Whisk in the 2 tablespoons extra-virgin olive oil and the capers and season with salt and black pepper.

5. Transfer the broccolini to a medium bowl, add the vinaigrette, and stir to combine. Let sit at room temperature for at least 15 minutes to allow the flavors to meld.

6. Reduce the oven temperature to 250°F.

7. Brush both sides of the arctic char with the remaining 2 tablespoons olive oil and season with salt and black pepper. Put in a small baking dish and bake until buttery and soft and just cooked through, about 15 minutes.

8. Transfer the arctic char to a platter and spoon the broccolini relish over the top.

Roasted Shrimp with Salsa Calabrese

SERVES 4

This recipe dusts shrimp with fennel and then roasts them until sweet and plump and serves them up with a Southern Italian–style sauce of meaty roasted eggplant, savory garlic and onions, sweet plum tomatoes, and, of course, spicy and fruity Calabrian pepper flakes.

4 Japanese eggplants (about 1 pound), peeled and diced

2 plum tomatoes, seeded and diced

1 red bell pepper, seeded and diced

1 small red onion, diced

4 garlic cloves, chopped

¼ to ½ teaspoon red pepper flakes, to taste, preferably Calabrian

5 tablespoons olive oil

Kosher salt and freshly ground black pepper

2 tablespoons red wine vinegar

¼ cup fresh basil, chopped, plus whole leaves for garnish

¼ cup fresh flat-leaf parsley, chopped

1 pound large (21- to 24-count) shrimp, peeled and deveined

1 teaspoon ground fennel

PER SERVING: Calories **333**; Protein **25g**; Carbohydrates **14g**; Dietary Fiber **6g**; Sugar **6g**; Total Fat **20g**; Saturated Fat **3g**

1. Preheat the oven to 425°F.

2. In a large bowl, combine the eggplant, tomatoes, bell pepper, onion, garlic, red pepper flakes, and 3 tablespoons of the oil, season with salt and black pepper, and toss to coat. Spread the vegetables on a large rimmed baking sheet and roast, stirring a few times, until soft and lightly golden brown, about 45 minutes. Remove from the oven and let cool for 10 minutes. Keep the oven on for the shrimp.

3. Transfer the vegetables to a food processor and puree until almost smooth. Add the vinegar and ¼ cup water, and continue processing until smooth. Add the basil and parsley and pulse a few times to incorporate while still leaving flecks of herbs, season with salt and black pepper, and transfer to a bowl. The vegetable sauce be made 1 day ahead and stored in a container with a lid in the refrigerator. Bring to room temperature before serving.

4. In a large bowl, toss the shrimp with the remaining 2 tablespoons oil and the fennel and season with salt and black pepper. Spread the shrimp in an even layer on a large rimmed baking sheet and roast, turning once, until pink and firm and just cooked through, about 8 minutes.

5. To serve, spoon some of the sauce into shallow bowls. Top each with about 5 shrimp and garnish with basil leaves.

Sautéed Shrimp with Spanish Bread Sauce

SERVES 4

½ cup olive oil

1 slice good-quality white bread sliced 1 inch thick, crusts removed, quartered

¾ cup Marcona almonds or California almonds

3 garlic cloves, smashed

¼ cup plus 2 tablespoons chopped fresh flat-leaf parsley

1 teaspoon Spanish paprika

1 teaspoon ground coriander

Kosher salt and freshly ground black pepper

1 pound large (21- to 24-count) shrimp, peeled and deveined

2 cups Best Vegetable Stock (page 140) or low-sodium store-bought

1 teaspoon finely chopped fresh thyme

1 tablespoon fresh lemon juice

PER SERVING: Calories **543**; Protein **24g**; Carbohydrates **15g**; Dietary Fiber **4g**; Sugar **7g**; Total Fat **42g**; Saturated Fat **4g**

This luscious one-pan meal, reminiscent of that garlicky favorite shrimp scampi, calls on a Spanish technique to enrich the sauce. Instead of butter or cream, an ingenious mixture of bread crumbs and roasted almonds is cooked in olive oil, pulsed to a paste in the food processor, and then added to veggie stock, rendering it thick and creamy. Preparing the sauce in the same pan used to sear the spice-crusted shrimp not only saves on dishes, but the browned bits that remain in the pan also add another layer of flavor and complexity to the sauce. This is excellent served with Salt-Roasted Potatoes (page 227) or over a bowl of quinoa or couscous.

1. In a large sauté pan, heat ¼ cup of the oil over medium heat until the oil begins to shimmer. Add the bread and cook until lightly golden brown on both sides. Remove to a plate lined with a paper towel to drain. Add the almonds to the pan and cook, stirring a few times, until lightly toasted and fragrant, about 2 minutes. Remove to the plate with the bread. Add the garlic to the pan and cook until lightly golden brown and slightly soft, about 2 minutes. Remove the garlic to the plate with the bread.

2. In a food processor, combine the bread, almonds, garlic, and ¼ cup of the parsley and process until you have a fine paste.

3. Add 2 tablespoons of the oil to the pan and heat the pan over high heat until the oil shimmers. In a medium bowl, combine the paprika, coriander, 2 teaspoons salt, and ½ teaspoon pepper. Add the shrimp to the bowl and toss well to coat. Cook the shrimp in batches in the hot pan until a crust has formed on one side, about 2 minutes. Turn over, cook for 1 minute longer, and remove to a plate (the shrimp will continue to cook in the sauce).

4. Add the remaining 2 tablespoons oil to the pan and heat over high heat until it shimmers. Add the almond paste and cook for 1 minute, stirring constantly. Add the stock and thyme, bring to a boil, and cook until it thickens to a sauce-like consistency, about 10 minutes. Stir the shrimp into the sauce, reduce the heat, and cook for 1 minute or until the shrimp are just cooked through. Season with salt and pepper, add the lemon juice, and mix in the remaining 2 tablespoons parsley.

Grilled Trout with Radicchio and Orange-Almond Vinaigrette

SERVES 4

2 oranges, halved

2 heads of radicchio, halved

3 tablespoons canola oil

Kosher salt and freshly ground black pepper

¼ cup finely chopped toasted blanched almonds

¼ cup balsamic vinegar

2 tablespoon chopped fresh flat-leaf parsley, plus whole leaves for garnish

1 teaspoon honey

1 teaspoon Dijon mustard

⅓ cup extra-virgin olive oil

4 (5-ounce) skin-on rainbow trout fillets, each about ½ inch thick

PER SERVING: Calories **584**; Protein **34g**; Carbohydrates **15g**; Dietary Fiber **2g**; Sugar **10g**; Total Fat **44g**; Saturated Fat **6g**

Trout amandine gets a makeover with the old butter-laden sauce giving way to a bright and juicy orange and almond vinaigrette. Grilling the oranges before juicing creates a roasted orange flavor that gives depth to the vinaigrette, the heightened sweetness balanced by sharp Dijon mustard. The almond-laced vinaigrette highlights the flavor of the trout while at the same time providing a nice counterpart to the bitter notes of grilled radicchio.

1. Heat a charcoal or gas grill to high for direct grilling or a grill pan over high heat on the stove.

2. Brush the cut sides of the oranges and radicchio with 2 tablespoons of the oil and season with salt and pepper. Put the oranges and radicchio cut side down on the grill and cook just until charred and slightly softened. Transfer the radicchio to a cutting board, coarsely chop, and put on a platter.

3. Squeeze the orange juice into a bowl and whisk in the almonds, vinegar, parsley, honey, mustard, and salt and pepper to taste. Slowly whisk in the olive oil until emulsified. Let sit at room temperature for at least 15 minutes before serving.

4. Brush the trout fillets with the remaining 1 tablespoon canola oil and sprinkle with salt and pepper on both sides. Grill until golden brown and slightly charred on both sides and just cooked through, about 3 minutes per side. Set atop the radicchio and immediately drizzle with the vinaigrette. Garnish with parsley leaves.

Grouper Steamed in Parchment with Martini Relish and Sour Orange Sauce

SERVES 2

Martini Relish

¼ cup quartered pitted green olives

2 jarred piquillo peppers, drained, patted dry, and diced

1 small shallot, thinly sliced

½ jalapeño pepper, finely diced

2 tablespoons extra-virgin olive oil

1 tablespoon white wine vinegar

2 tablespoons finely chopped fresh flat-leaf parsley

Kosher salt and freshly ground black pepper

Grouper

2 (5-ounce) skinless grouper fillets

Kosher salt and freshly ground black pepper

2 tablespoons extra-virgin olive oil

2 tablespoons dry white wine

Sour Orange Sauce (recipe follows)

PER SERVING (INCLUDES SAUCE):
Calories **589**; Protein **30g**;
Carbohydrates **43g**; Dietary Fiber **2g**;
Sugar **7g**; Total Fat **32g**; Saturated
Fat **4g**

Sour orange sauce is a seriously simple way to grace your dish with intense, lip-smacking flavor. Add to that a slightly spicy, briny green olive relish (gotta love the piquillo peppers standing in for old-school martini olive pimientos) and an otherwise unassuming piece of mild grouper is transformed into a flavor-packed home run of a dish. Baking in parchment is a great way to impart lots of flavor, not fat, into your fish. I call for a combination of orange and lime juices to mimic the sweet-sour citrus, but if you can find sour oranges by all means use them for an additional wild, almost floral note.

1. Make the relish: In a bowl, combine the olives, piquillo peppers, shallot, jalapeño, oil, vinegar, parsley, and salt and black pepper to taste. Let sit at room temperature for at least 15 minutes to allow the flavors to meld.

2. Cook the fish: Preheat the oven to 400°F. Cut two 12½ × 16-inch squares of parchment paper.

3. Sprinkle the fillets on both sides with salt and black pepper. Put 1 fillet in the center of each piece of parchment paper. Top each fillet with 1 tablespoon oil and 1 tablespoon wine. Fold the edges together by tightly crimping around all sides to seal the packets completely. Put the packets on a baking sheet or in a large ovenproof sauté pan. Bake for 15 minutes, until the fish is cooked through.

4. Put each packet on a dinner plate and let sit for 2 minutes. Then open the parchment and drizzle with sour orange sauce and top with the martini relish.

Sour Orange Sauce

MAKES ABOUT ⅓ CUP

2 cups fresh orange juice

1 tablespoon honey

Juice of 1 lime

2 teaspoons white wine vinegar

Kosher salt and freshly ground
  black pepper

In a small nonreactive saucepan, bring the orange juice to a boil over high heat, and cook until thickened and reduced to about ¼ cup. Whisk in the honey and transfer to a bowl. Whisk in the lime juice and vinegar, and season with salt and pepper. The sauce can be stored, covered in the refrigerator, for up to 3 days.

PER 2 TABLESPOONS:
Calories **120**; Protein **1g**; Carbohydrates **29g**; Dietary Fiber **0g**; Sugar **27g**; Total Fat **0g**; Saturated Fat **0g**

Cod in Spicy Ginger Broth with Mushrooms and Cockles

SERVES 4

1 tablespoon plus 1 teaspoon olive oil

2 shallots, sliced paper thin

2 to 3 tablespoons grated peeled fresh ginger, to taste

2 garlic cloves, sliced paper thin

12 New Zealand cockles, shells rinsed well

1 cup dry sake

1 (20-ounce) skinless cod fillet

Kosher salt and freshly ground black pepper

2 tablespoons white miso

2 teaspoons low-sodium tamari

6 shiitake mushrooms, stems removed, caps thinly sliced

2 large oyster mushrooms, thinly sliced

Juice of 1 lime

1 large bunch of enoki mushrooms, pulled apart

¼ cup fresh cilantro, chopped

2 tablespoons chopped fresh flat-leaf parsley

PER SERVING: Calories **325**; Protein **32g**; Carbohydrates **18g**; Dietary Fiber **3g**; Sugar **8g**; Total Fat **7g**; Saturated Fat **1g**; Alcohol **10g**

This broth is beyond flavorful; its briny, savory, acidic, and sweetly spicy elements come together in a balanced harmony that brings to mind the same rush of the first taste of Chinese hot-and-sour soup. It's a restorative dish, so clean and energizing that you can practically feel your body thanking you with each delicious bite. I like to make this with sweet, mild cod, baked in the oven until just flaky, but tofu would also be an appropriate pairing. Top with Pickled Saffron Shallots (page 34) for an extra pop of color and flavor.

1. Preheat the oven to 375°F.

2. Heat 1 tablespoon of the oil in a large Dutch oven over medium-high heat until it begins to shimmer. Add the shallots and ginger and cook until they are soft without color, 2 to 3 minutes. Add the garlic and cook for another minute. Add the cockles and sauté for 1 minute. Pour in the sake and cover with a tight-fitting lid. After about 2 minutes, check to see if the cockles have opened. As soon as the cockles open, carefully transfer them to a plate, emptying any of their liquor back into the pan. (Discard any that do not open.)

3. Put the cod fillet on a rimmed baking sheet lined with parchment paper. Using a pastry brush, brush the remaining 1 teaspoon olive oil on top of the fish and season with salt and pepper. Bake the fish for about 10 minutes, until it's flaky and just cooked through.

4. While the cod is roasting, whisk 2 cups water, the miso paste, and the tamari into the cooking liquid in the pot. Bring to a boil, then reduce the heat to low, and simmer for 2 minutes to let the flavors meld. Taste and add salt, as needed.

5. Add the shiitake and oyster mushrooms to the broth and let them cook for about 3 minutes. Stir the lime juice into the broth and scatter the enoki mushrooms around just to let them wilt slightly. Add the cockles back to the pan and garnish with the cilantro and parsley.

6. Using a fish spatula, remove the fish from the pan, transfer it to the pot with the broth, and serve.

Chicken Adobo with Mustard-Marinated Kale

SERVES 6

2 cups fresh orange juice

2 teaspoons ancho chile powder

2 teaspoons New Mexico chile powder

1 teaspoon garlic powder

1 teaspoon onion powder

1 teaspoon dried oregano, preferably Mexican

½ teaspoon ground cumin

4 (8-ounce) boneless, skinless chicken breast halves

2 tablespoons canola oil

Kosher salt and freshly ground black pepper

Mustard-Marinated Kale Salad (page 133)

PER SERVING: Calories **394**; Protein **38g**; Carbohydrates **14g**; Dietary Fiber **4g**; Sugar **4g**; Total Fat **21g**; Saturated Fat **3g**

I have been making this recipe since my days at Miracle Grill. I don't necessarily want to own up to just how long that's been, but let's just say Chicken Adobo is a classic! Back in the day, I used to serve it with spinach sautéed in about a pound of butter. This hearty kale salad goes just as well and is a far-better-for-you option. Aces all around.

1. In a medium baking dish, whisk together the orange juice, chile powders, garlic powder, onion powder, oregano, and cumin until combined. Add the chicken and turn to coat. Cover and marinate, turning a few times, in the refrigerator for at least 6 hours and up to 24 hours. The longer you allow the chicken to marinate, the more flavorful it will become.

2. In a large sauté pan, heat the oil over high heat until it begins to shimmer. Remove the chicken from the marinade, allowing excess to run off. Season each breast on both sides with salt and pepper. Add the chicken to the pan, top side up, and cook until golden brown, about 4 minutes. Flip the chicken over and cook until the bottom is lightly golden brown and the chicken is cooked through, about 4 minutes.

3. Remove the chicken from the pan, tent loosely with foil, and let rest for 5 minutes. Slice the chicken into thick slices on the bias and serve alongside the kale.

Spanish Spiced Chicken Breast with Spicy Mint Sauce

SERVES 4

Chicken

2 tablespoons Spanish paprika

2 teaspoons ground cumin

2 teaspoons dry mustard

2 teaspoons ground fennel

4 (5-ounce) boneless, skinless chicken breast halves, lightly pounded

2 tablespoons extra-virgin olive oil

Kosher salt and freshly ground black pepper

Spicy Mint Sauce

1½ cups (packed) fresh flat-leaf parsley

½ cup (packed) fresh mint

2 garlic cloves, coarsely chopped

1 serrano pepper, seeded and coarsely chopped

1 tablespoon honey

2 tablespoons Dijon mustard

⅓ cup extra-virgin olive oil

Kosher salt and freshly ground black pepper

PER SERVING: Calories **416**; Protein **34g**; Carbohydrates **7g**; Dietary Fiber **1g**; Sugar **4g**; Total Fat **28g**; Saturated Fat **4g**

This recipe used to be on the dinner menu at Bolo, and every time I make it for people at my home they can't get over how chicken seasoned with pantry spices can be so incredibly delicious and good for you. Serve with Broccoli Salad with Anchovy and Vinegar (page 202) or Roasted Broccoli with Roasted Lemon and Parmesan (page 204) and a simple cooked grain.

1. Cook the chicken: In a small bowl, combine the paprika, cumin, mustard, and fennel. Brush the chicken on both sides with the oil and season on both sides with salt and black pepper. Rub the top side with the rub; let sit at room temperature for 15 minutes.

2. Heat a grill pan over medium heat. Cook the chicken, rub side down, in the pan until a crust has formed, about 4 minutes; turn over and continue cooking until just cooked through, about 4 minutes longer. Transfer the chicken to plates or a platter, tent loosely with foil, and let rest for 5 minutes.

3. While the chicken is cooking, make the sauce: In a food processor, pulse the parsley, mint, garlic, and serrano until coarsely chopped. Add the honey and mustard and pulse again until combined. With the motor running, slowly add the olive oil until the mixture has become emulsified. Transfer the mixture to a bowl, and if necessary, whisk in a few tablespoons of water to thin the sauce. Season with salt and black pepper to taste.

4. Spoon some of the sauce over each chicken breast, and serve, with the remaining sauce on the side.

Quinoa con Pollo with Peas and Green Olives

SERVES 4

1 cup pitted green olives, thinly sliced

¼ cup chopped fresh cilantro or flat-leaf parsley, plus whole leaves for garnish

2 tablespoons red wine vinegar

Pinch of red pepper flakes, preferably Calabrian

2 (8-ounce) boneless, skinless chicken breast halves

2 tablespoons Adobo Seasoning (page 36)

4 tablespoons olive oil

1 Spanish onion, halved and thinly sliced

1 red bell pepper, halved, seeded, and thinly sliced

1 yellow bell pepper, halved, seeded, and thinly sliced

1 jalapeño pepper, finely diced

2 cups Best Chicken Stock (page 141) or low-sodium store-bought

Kosher salt and freshly ground black pepper

1 cup quinoa

1 bay leaf

1 cup frozen peas, thawed

PER SERVING: Calories **524**; Protein **36g**; Carbohydrates **46g**; Dietary Fiber **6g**; Sugar **6g**; Total Fat **22g**; Saturated Fat **3g**

This recipe is my version of Puerto Rican arroz con pollo, deconstructed and nutrient-boosted. Rice is delicious, and while there's nothing unhealthy about it per se, there is a whole other world of power grains out there that can step in and bring a lot more nutrition to the table—like quinoa. This dish preserves all the great sofrito-boosted flavor of the original, trust me.

1. In a bowl, combine the olives, cilantro, vinegar, and red pepper flakes and let sit at room temperature for at least 30 minutes.

2. Season the chicken breasts on both sides with the adobo seasoning and let sit at room temperature for 15 minutes.

3. In a medium saucepan, heat 2 tablespoons of the oil over medium heat. Add the onion, bell peppers, and jalapeño and cook until soft, about 4 minutes. Add the stock, 1 teaspoon salt, and ⅛ teaspoon black pepper and bring to a boil. Stir in the quinoa and bay leaf. Cover, reduce the heat, and simmer for 15 minutes.

4. Stir the peas into the quinoa and continue to simmer until the quinoa is tender and the liquid has been absorbed, about 5 minutes more. Let sit for 10 minutes and fluff with a fork. Discard the bay leaf.

5. While the quinoa is cooking, heat the remaining 2 tablespoons oil in a large nonstick sauté pan over high heat until it begins to shimmer. Add the chicken and cook on both sides until golden brown and just cooked through, about 9 minutes total. Remove from the heat and let rest for 5 minutes before cutting into ½-inch-thick slices on the bias.

6. Spoon the quinoa into bowls, top with slices of the chicken, and top with the green olive mixture. Garnish with fresh herbs.

Poached Chicken with Salsa Verde

SERVES 6

Chicken

1 (4-pound) whole chicken, rinsed and patted dry, backbone removed and reserved

4 cups Best Chicken Stock (page 141) or low-sodium store-bought

1 cup fruity white wine

1 head of garlic, split in half crosswise

8 fresh thyme sprigs

1 small bunch of fresh flat-leaf parsley

12 black peppercorns

1 lemon, halved

2 teaspoons kosher salt

Salsa Verde

2 garlic cloves

5 anchovy fillets

2 tablespoons capers, drained and chopped

½ cup extra-virgin olive oil

Pinch of red pepper flakes, preferably Calabrian

1 cup fresh flat-leaf parsley, finely chopped

½ cup fresh tarragon, finely chopped

¼ cup thinly sliced fresh chives

Kosher salt and freshly ground black pepper

2 tablespoons aged sherry vinegar

PER SERVING: Calories **315**; Protein **26g**; Carbohydrates **1g**; Dietary Fiber **0g**; Sugar **0g**; Total Fat **22g**; Saturated Fat **3g**

Poaching gets a bad rap, possibly because most people just toss fish or chicken or vegetables into plain water and cook them to death just like that. When you use a tasty broth spiked with herbs and spices, you can add so much flavor to the main ingredient—in this case, chicken. I serve a version of this dish at Gato in New York City, but this is a less indulgent version perfect for making at home. A bright salsa verde, brimming with parsley, tarragon, chives, and a touch of heat, perks up the whole dish.

1. Poach the chicken: Put the chicken and the backbone in a large pot and add the stock, wine, and enough cold water to cover the chicken by 1 inch. Add the garlic, thyme, parsley, peppercorns, lemon, and salt. Put a heat-proof plate on top to keep the chicken submerged in the liquid. Bring to a boil over high heat and cook for 5 minutes. Remove from the heat, cover, and let sit for 1 hour.

2. Meanwhile, make the salsa verde: On a cutting board, combine the garlic and anchovies and chop until you have a fine paste. Transfer to a small bowl, add the capers, oil, and red pepper flakes, and mix to combine. Stir in the parsley, tarragon, and chives and season with salt and black pepper. Let sit at room temperature until ready to serve or for up to an hour or two. Stir in the vinegar just before serving.

3. Remove the chicken from the poaching liquid and transfer to a bowl. Cover loosely to keep warm. Strain 3 cups of the poaching liquid into a medium saucepan, bring to a boil, and cook until reduced by half and the flavors intensify, about 25 minutes.

4. Meanwhile, remove the skin from the chicken and slice or use your hands to pull apart into big pieces. Serve the chicken in bowls and top each with a ladle of the reduced poaching liquid and a heaping spoonful of the salsa verde.

Roast Chicken Dinner with Mustard Greens and Torn Rye Bread Croutons

SERVES 8

This meal is probably at the top of many people's list of most comforting dinners, especially in the fall or winter. My recipe takes inspiration from the divine chicken made famous by the late, great Judy Rogers at her Zuni Café in San Francisco. Baby mustard greens add a subtle peppery bite and kumquats lend sweetness and an appealing slight bitterness. If you can't find kumquats, orange segments will work perfectly instead.

Chicken

1 (4-pound) whole chicken, rinsed well and patted dry

Kosher salt and freshly ground black pepper

6 fresh thyme sprigs

6 fresh tarragon sprigs

2 garlic cloves

½ lemon

Salad

4 (½-inch-thick) slices good day-old rye bread or 12-grain bread, crusts removed, torn into 1-inch pieces

2 tablespoons Dijon mustard

3 tablespoons red wine vinegar

Juice of 1 lemon

2 tablespoons extra-virgin olive oil

Kosher salt and freshly ground black pepper

Red pepper flakes, preferably Calabrian (optional)

4 ounces baby mustard greens

1 head of frisée, snipped into bite-size pieces

2 inner celery ribs and leaves, thinly sliced

8 kumquats, halved, cut crosswise into thin slices, and seeded

5 fresh tarragon leaves, chopped

PER SERVING: Calories 272; Protein 21g; Carbohydrates 13g; Dietary Fiber 2g; Sugar 1g; Total Fat 15g; Saturated Fat 4g

1. Roast the chicken: Season the chicken inside and out, on all sides, with salt and pepper. Stuff the thyme, tarragon, garlic cloves, and lemon half inside the cavity. Put the chicken breast side down in a shallow baking dish and lightly blanket the chicken with paper towels (do not tightly seal in plastic wrap as you want the skin to dry out so that it is crispier when baking). Refrigerate for at least 4 hours and up to 24 hours.

2. Preheat the oven to 400°F. Put a large, empty cast-iron skillet into the oven as it preheats.

3. When ready to roast, using potholders, remove the skillet from the oven and carefully set the chicken, breast side down, into the hot skillet. Return the skillet to the oven and roast the chicken for 30 minutes.

4. After 30 minutes, carefully flip the chicken (I suggest gripping it from the cavity with a pair of kitchen tongs) and return it to the oven to roast until cooked through, about 25 minutes more.

5. Remove the pan from oven and let the chicken rest in the pan for 10 minutes. Carefully transfer the chicken to a plate, tent loosely with foil, and continue to rest for an additional 10 minutes before serving. Pour the collected chicken drippings into a heat-proof container and set aside for the vinaigrette.

6. Start the salad: Put the bread in the skillet and return it to the oven. Toast, stirring once or twice, until the croutons are lightly golden brown and crispy, about 7 minutes. Transfer the bread to a plate. Pour ¼ cup water into the pan and scrape up any bits stuck to the bottom of the pan; reserve.

(Recipe continues)

7. In a medium bowl, whisk together the mustard, vinegar, and lemon juice. Slowly drizzle in the olive oil, whisking to emulsify. Season with salt and black pepper and red pepper flakes, if desired. Continue whisking, slowly adding the chicken drippings into the vinaigrette as well as the water mixture from the skillet. Taste and re-season as needed.

8. Put the greens in a large bowl. Add the celery, kumquats, tarragon, and croutons, season with salt and black pepper, and toss to distribute. Dress the salad with 3 tablespoons of the vinaigrette and toss to coat. Add additional vinaigrette as needed. Transfer to a platter.

9. Cut the chicken into pieces and serve on top of the salad, with extra dressing on the side.

Lamb Loin Shawarma with Green Harissa Yogurt and Pickled Vegetables

SERVES 8

1 (2-pound) lamb loin, trimmed of fat

3 garlic cloves, thinly sliced

¼ cup olive oil

2 teaspoons ground sumac

2 teaspoons ground cumin

½ teaspoon ground cinnamon

¼ teaspoon cayenne powder

2 tablespoons light brown sugar

1 cup 2% Greek yogurt

Finely grated zest of 1 lime

¼ cup Green Harissa (page 28)

8 whole-wheat pita or homemade Yogurt Flatbread (page 119), warmed

½ cup pickled vegetables (such as red onion, radish, or shallot; see pages 32–34)

PER SERVING: Calories **459**; Protein **26g**; Carbohydrates **37g**; Dietary Fiber **5g**; Sugar **2g**; Total Fat **24g**; Saturated Fat **9g**

A little like a taco, a lot like a gyro, shawarma is a Lebanese dish of spit-roasted meat thinly sliced, slathered in yogurt sauce, and wrapped in flatbread. Stacks of meat are layered in an inverted cone, so the fat can run down and hit each part as the meat rotates—it's pretty impressive. A tender, lean loin of lamb, crusted in rich Middle Eastern spices, seared, and roasted, delivers a comparable experience with a lot less fat. Green harissa, herbaceous and bright, pairs with thick Greek yogurt for a creamy, flavorful sauce.

1. Using a small paring knife, make small slits all over the surface of the lamb loin. Stuff each slit with a thin slice of the garlic.

2. In a 9-inch baking dish, whisk together the oil, sumac, cumin, cinnamon, cayenne, and brown sugar until smooth. Add the lamb, turn to coat, and then cover, and let marinate for at least 30 minutes and up to 2 hours in the refrigerator.

3. Preheat the oven to 400°F. Remove the lamb from the refrigerator 30 minutes before cooking to bring to room temperature.

4. Heat an ovenproof skillet, preferably cast iron, over medium heat until smoking. Add the lamb and sear on all sides until browned, about 5 minutes. Transfer to the oven and continue cooking until the internal temperature reaches 135°F, about 10 minutes.

5. Remove the lamb to a cutting board and let rest for 10 minutes. Slice thin.

6. Put the yogurt in a bowl. Mix the lime zest into the harissa and then swirl the mixture into the yogurt.

7. Serve slices of lamb stuffed into or on top of the pita, topped with the green harissa yogurt and pickled vegetables.

Spanish Spice–Rubbed Lamb Loin with Mustard-Mint Glaze

SERVES 4

1¼ pounds lamb loin, trimmed of fat

Kosher salt and freshly ground black pepper

2 heaping tablespoons Spanish Spice Rub (page 36)

3 tablespoons pure olive oil

½ cup Mustard-Mint Glaze (page 27)

PER SERVING: Calories **439**; Protein **28g**; Carbohydrates **7g**; Dietary Fiber **1g**; Sugar **5g**; Total Fat **33g**; Saturated Fat **10g**

Lamb loin is a favorite of mine, and I find that even those who claim not to like the flavor of lamb are happy to tuck into a plate of this cut, especially when crusted with this ruddy Spanish spice rub and drizzled with a mustardy honey glaze. And the mint—well, not only does it make such a nice counterpart to the sweet-sharp flavors in play, it's practically a must-pair with lamb. This springtime dish would be the perfect centerpiece for your Easter or Passover table. Serve with farro (see page 46) and crumbled herbed goat cheese mixed with chopped fresh mint.

1. Preheat the oven to 425°F.

2. Season both sides of each loin with salt and pepper and rub one side of each loin with some of the spice rub.

3. Heat the oil in a large ovenproof sauté pan over medium-high heat until it begins to shimmer. Put the lamb in the pan, rub side down, and cook until golden brown and a crust has formed, about 3 minutes. Flip the lamb over and transfer to the oven until cooked to medium-rare (an internal temperature of 135°F), about 8 minutes.

4. Remove from the oven, tent loosely with foil, and let rest for 5 minutes before slicing. Serve slices drizzled with the glaze.

Lamb-Chickpea Patties with Mustard Seed Chermoula

SERVES 6

4 tablespoons olive oil

½ medium red onion, grated

1 garlic clove, chopped

⅛ teaspoon ground allspice

⅛ teaspoon ground cumin

⅛ teaspoon ground coriander

Pinch of cayenne powder

Kosher salt and freshly ground black pepper

1 cup canned chickpeas, drained, rinsed, and drained again

3 tablespoons finely chopped fresh mint

3 tablespoons finely chopped fresh flat-leaf parsley

Finely grated zest of 1 lemon

2 tablespoons fresh lemon juice

¾ pound ground 90% lean lamb

¾ cup Mustard Seed Chermoula (recipe follows)

PER SERVING (INCLUDES SAUCE): Calories **440**; Protein **16g**; Carbohydrates **14g**; Dietary Fiber **5g**; Sugar **1g**; Total Fat **36g**; Saturated Fat **8g**

Think of this as a Moroccan burger, highly seasoned with layers of smoky spices, fresh herbs, and bright lemon. Adding chickpeas, so often used in Moroccan cuisine, is a great way to stretch a mere three quarters of a pound of ground lamb into enough patties to feed six with ease. Italy has its pesto, Argentina its chimichurri, and Morocco has chermoula, though this pungent herb sauce is flavored as much by the spices it contains—cumin, coriander, and, in this version, mustard seeds—as by the leaves of cilantro and parsley that give it its bright color.

1. In a small sauté pan, heat 2 tablespoons of the oil over medium heat until it shimmers. Add the onion and garlic and cook until soft, 2 minutes. Add the allspice, cumin, coriander, and cayenne and cook for 30 seconds; season with salt and pepper. Add ½ cup water and cook until it has evaporated almost completely. Let cool slightly.

2. In a food processor, combine the chickpeas with the onion mixture, mint, parsley, and lemon zest and juice, and season with salt and pepper. Process until coarsely ground.

3. Put the lamb in a large bowl, season with salt and pepper, and add the chickpea mixture. Gently mix to combine. Cover and refrigerate for at least 30 minutes and up to 4 hours to allow the patties to chill and the flavors to meld.

4. Heat the remaining 2 tablespoons oil in a large cast-iron pan until it shimmers. Form the lamb mixture into 6 even patties, each about ½ inch thick, and season on both sides with salt and pepper. Cook the patties until golden brown and just cooked through, about 4 minutes per side.

5. Serve the patties topped with the chermoula.

Mustard Seed Chermoula

MAKES ABOUT 1 CUP

1 teaspoon brown mustard seeds

1 tablespoon olive oil

2 garlic cloves, chopped to a paste

2 teaspoons ground cumin

½ teaspoon ground coriander

1 teaspoon sweet paprika

1 cup fresh cilantro

1 cup fresh flat-leaf parsley

½ cup extra-virgin olive oil

¼ cup fresh lemon juice

⅛ teaspoon cayenne powder

Kosher salt and freshly ground
  black pepper

1. Heat a small sauté pan over low heat, add the mustard seeds, and lightly toast, shaking the pan constantly, until the seeds are fragrant, about 2 minutes. Set aside on a plate to cool.

2. Heat the oil in the same pan over medium heat. Add the garlic and cook until soft, about 30 seconds. Add the cumin, coriander, and paprika and cook for 1 minute. Add ½ cup water and cook, stirring, until a paste forms. Remove from the heat and set aside to cool.

3. In a food processor, combine the cilantro and parsley and process until finely chopped. In a medium bowl, mix together the olive oil, lemon juice, cayenne, garlic paste, and mustard seeds. Stir in the herbs and season with salt and pepper. Let sit at room temperature for at least 30 minutes before serving, or cover and refrigerate for up to 8 hours. Bring to room temperature before serving.

PER 2 TABLESPOONS:
Calories **150**; Protein **0g**; Carbohydrates **2g**; Dietary Fiber **0g**; Sugar **0g**; Total Fat **16g**; Saturated Fat **2g**

Pomegranate and Chile Glazed Pork Carnitas

SERVES 8

1 cup pomegranate or cranberry juice

2 tablespoons pomegranate molasses

1 tablespoon pureed canned chipotle in adobo

Kosher salt and freshly ground black pepper

2 tablespoons ancho chile powder

1 teaspoon ground coriander

2 pounds pork tenderloin

2 tablespoons canola oil

1 head of Boston lettuce, separated into leaves

½ cup Pickled Red Onions (page 32)

1½ cups Guacamole (page 25)

¼ cup pomegranate seeds

PER SERVING: Calories **259**; Protein **24g**; Carbohydrates **14g**; Dietary Fiber **2g**; Sugar **9g**; Total Fat **12g**; Saturated Fat **2g**

Carnitas, those juicy, perfectly fried crunchy pieces of pork served in every Mexican restaurant across the country, are simply delicioso—and pretty caloric. Here is a version that has all of the same flavors but uses a leaner cut of meat, the tenderloin. Another way to make this dish fit-friendly is to use tender leaves of Boston lettuce to wrap the morsels of pork in place of the traditional tortillas. There's no substitute for smooth guacamole, though, so that stays in place, with pickled red onions and ruby pomegranate seeds to finish the dish in style.

1. In a small saucepan, combine the pomegranate juice, molasses, and chipotle, season with salt and pepper, and bring to a boil over high heat. Cook until reduced by half, about 15 minutes. Remove from the heat.

2. Preheat the oven to 425°F.

3. In a small bowl, mix together the chile powder, coriander, 2 teaspoons salt, and ½ teaspoon pepper. Season the loin with the spice mix, rubbing it in so that it adheres, and let sit at room temperature for 15 minutes.

4. Heat the oil in a large ovenproof nonstick sauté pan or cast-iron pan over high heat. Sear the pork on all sides until a crust forms, about 2 minutes per side. Transfer to the oven and cook until medium (an internal temperature of 145°F), about 12 minutes.

5. Transfer the pork to a cutting board, tent loosely with foil, and let rest for 10 minutes. Cut into 1-inch dice and toss in the pomegranate sauce.

6. Serve the pork in lettuce leaves topped with pickled red onions, guacamole, and pomegranate seeds.

Basil-Rubbed Grilled Pork Tenderloin with Peach Mostarda

SERVES 8

Peaches, pork, and mustard are all flavors that were born to be together. Pork tenderloin is an especially lean cut, and pairing it with flavors and ingredients that taste good without the need for extra fat and calories is my idea of fit food. Nectarines are a perfect, seasonally appropriate sub for peaches, and for another simple variation, rubbing the pork with rosemary instead of basil works nicely, too.

Peach Mostarda

1 pound very ripe peaches, peeled, pitted, and diced

2 tablespoons sugar

1 teaspoon finely grated orange zest

1 teaspoon finely grated lemon zest

Juice of ½ orange

Juice of 1 lemon

2 tablespoons dry white wine

1 tablespoon dry mustard

¼ teaspoon kosher salt

⅛ teaspoon freshly ground black pepper

1 teaspoon coriander seeds

1 teaspoon mustard seeds

1 teaspoon finely chopped fresh rosemary

2 tablespoons whole-grain mustard

1 ripe white peach, peeled, pitted, and finely diced

Pork

2 pounds pork tenderloin, excess fat trimmed

8 fresh basil leaves, plus additional sprigs for garnish

2 tablespoons olive oil

Kosher salt and freshly ground black pepper

PER SERVING: Calories **244**; Protein **26g**; Carbohydrates **13g**; Dietary Fiber **2g**; Sugar **11g**; Total Fat **9g**; Saturated Fat **2g**

1. Make the mostarda: In a medium, nonreactive saucepan, combine the peaches and the sugar and let macerate for 15 minutes.

2. In a small bowl, whisk together the orange zest, lemon zest, orange juice, lemon juice, wine, dry mustard, salt, and pepper.

3. Toast the coriander seeds and mustard seeds in a small dry sauté pan over medium heat until just fragrant, about 1 minute.

4. Add the coriander seeds, mustard seeds, rosemary, and juice mixture to the peaches and cook over high heat until the mixture comes to a boil, about 8 minutes. Reduce the heat to medium and continue to cook, stirring occasionally, until the mixture thickens and has a jam-like consistency, about 15 minutes longer.

5. Remove from the heat and let cool for 10 minutes. Whisk in the whole-grain mustard and the chopped white peach. Once cool, the mostarda can be covered and refrigerated overnight. Serve at room temperature.

6. Grill the pork: Preheat the grill to high or a grill pan over high heat.

7. Rub the entire tenderloin with the basil leaves. Let sit at room temperature for 15 minutes. Brush with the oil and season with salt and pepper.

8. Grill the pork, turning as needed, until golden brown and slightly charred and an instant-read thermometer inserted into the center registers 140°F, 15 to 18 minutes. Remove from the grill, tent loosely with foil, and let the pork rest for 10 minutes before slicing into 1-inch-thick slices. Serve with peach mostarda on the side.

Grilled Skirt Steak with Tomato-Horseradish Salsa

SERVES 4

Tomato-Horseradish Salsa

3 tablespoons red wine vinegar

1 tablespoon fresh lemon juice

2 tablespoons prepared horseradish, drained

A few dashes of Worcestershire sauce

¼ teaspoon freshly ground black pepper

1 pint cherry tomatoes, halved

½ celery stalk, thinly sliced, plus celery leaves, chopped

½ red onion, thinly sliced

2 pickled jalapeño peppers (see page 32), thinly sliced

¼ cup chopped fresh cilantro

Steak

1 pound 4 ounces skirt steak

2 tablespoons canola oil

Kosher salt and freshly ground black pepper

¼ cup Steak Rub (page 37)

PER SERVING: Calories **346**; Protein **32g**; Carbohydrates **9g**; Dietary Fiber **3g**; Sugar **3g**; Total Fat **20g**; Saturated Fat **5g**

You don't need to wait for the weekend for a Bloody Mary fix—take all of the ingredients typically included in that brunch cocktail and transform them into a spicy, savory salsa to spoon over a perfectly grilled, spice-rubbed skirt steak. Crazy delicious, zero hangover.

1. Make the salsa: In a medium bowl, whisk together the vinegar, lemon juice, horseradish, Worcestershire, and black pepper. Add the tomatoes, celery stalk and leaves, onion, jalapeños, and cilantro and let sit at room temperature for at least 30 minutes before serving.

2. Grill the steak: Brush the steak on both sides with the oil and season with salt and black pepper. Season the top side with the rub. Let sit at room temperature for 30 minutes.

3. Preheat the grill to high or a grill pan over high heat.

4. Grill the steak on both sides until golden brown and cooked to medium-rare, about 12 minutes total. Remove from the grill, tent loosely with foil, and let rest for 5 minutes before slicing on the bias into thin slices. Top with the salsa.

Kalbi-Style Flank Steak with Cucumber Kimchi in Lettuce Leaves

SERVES 6

I learned to make this recipe from a Korean woman on the set of my show *Grill It!* many years ago. It achieves that perfect balance of sweet, salty, and spicy, with some fresh and crunchy elements to boot. With tons of spice, this dish is so flavorful that a little goes a long way. Satisfaction guaranteed.

Steak

¼ cup low-sodium tamari or soy sauce

1 tablespoon toasted sesame oil

1 small ripe Asian pear, peeled and grated

1 tablespoon gochujang (chile paste)

1 tablespoon honey or pure maple syrup

2 garlic cloves, chopped

1 tablespoon finely grated peeled fresh ginger

1½ pounds flank steak

Cucumber Kimchi

½ cup rice wine vinegar

2 tablespoons low-sodium tamari or soy sauce

2 teaspoons sugar

2 teaspoons finely grated peeled fresh ginger

1 tablespoon gochujang (chile paste), or more to taste

1 teaspoon toasted sesame oil

4 Kirby cucumbers, thinly sliced

1 small white onion, thinly sliced

1 tablespoon toasted sesame seeds

2 heads of butter lettuce, leaves separated

Fresh cilantro, for garnish

1. Marinate the steak: In a small bowl, whisk together the tamari, sesame oil, pear, gochujang, honey, garlic, and ginger. Put the steak in a baking dish, add the marinade, and turn to coat. Cover and marinate in the refrigerator for at least 4 hours and up to 24 hours. Remove from the refrigerator 30 minutes before grilling.

2. Make the kimchi: In a medium bowl, whisk together the vinegar, tamari, sugar, ginger, gochujang, and sesame oil. Add the cucumbers, onion, and sesame seeds and toss to combine. Cover and refrigerate for at least 1 hour and up to 8 hours.

3. Grill the steak: Heat the grill to high or a grill pan over high heat.

4. Remove the steak from the marinade and pat dry with paper towels. Grill until both sides are golden brown and the steak is cooked to medium-rare, about 12 minutes. Remove from the grill, tent loosely with foil, and let rest for 10 minutes before slicing against the grain. Serve in lettuce leaves topped with the cucumber kimchi. Garnish with cilantro.

PER SERVING: Calories **239**; Protein **24g**; Carbohydrates **6g**; Dietary Fiber **0g**; Sugar **4g**; Total Fat **13g**; Saturated Fat **5g**

Orange Beef and Garlic-Roasted Greens and Brown Rice

SERVES 4

4 tablespoons canola oil

3 garlic cloves, finely smashed to a paste

3-inch piece of fresh ginger, peeled and finely grated

Pinch of red pepper flakes, preferably Calabrian, or 1 tablespoon garlic red chile paste

2 long strips orange zest

2 cups fresh orange juice

2 tablespoons low-sodium soy sauce

1 tablespoon honey

1¼ pounds flank steak, cut in half crosswise

2 portobello mushrooms, cut in half and then sliced crosswise into ¼-inch-thick slices

Freshly ground black pepper

Garlic-Roasted Greens and Brown Rice (recipe follows)

¼ cup fresh cilantro

PER SERVING (INCLUDES GREENS AND RICE): Calories **471**; Protein **34g**; Carbohydrates **39g**; Dietary Fiber **5g**; Sugar **7g**; Total Fat **20g**; Saturated Fat **5g**

My 1970s youth included its fair share of Orange Beef and Broccoli served up with white rice from my beloved local Chinese delivery joint. Man, was it delicious. I ran track; it didn't matter to me then that the beef was deep-fried and then stir-fried with the broccoli in more oil before it was all swathed in a cornstarch-thickened sauce. Here's a lighter yet still very flavorful version of that classic dish.

1. In a medium saucepan, heat 2 tablespoons of the oil over medium heat until it shimmers. Add the garlic and ginger and cook until softened but not browned, 1 minute. Add the red pepper flakes and cook for 10 seconds. Add the orange zest and juice, return to a simmer, and cook until the liquid has reduced by half. Whisk in the soy sauce and honey. Remove the glaze from the heat and let cool completely. It will thicken as it cools. The glaze can be made 24 hours in advance, covered, and refrigerated.

2. Remove ¼ cup of the glaze and reserve. Put the steak in a large zip-top plastic bag, add the remaining orange glaze, and mix around to coat. Refrigerate for at least 4 hours and up to 24 hours.

3. Remove the steak from the refrigerator and let sit at room temperature for 30 minutes before cooking.

4. In a large cast-iron skillet or nonstick pan, heat the remaining 2 tablespoons oil over high heat. Cook the mushrooms in batches until golden brown and cooked through, about 8 minutes. Transfer to a plate.

5. Add the beef to the pan in batches and cook over high heat until golden brown on the bottom, about 4 minutes. Turn over and continue cooking to medium-rare, about 5 minutes longer. Remove from the pan and let rest for 5 minutes before slicing against the grain.

6. Serve the rice and greens in bowls and top with the beef and mushrooms. Drizzle with the reserved glaze and add some cilantro leaves.

Garlic-Roasted Greens and Brown Rice

SERVES 6

1½ tablespoons canola oil

2 garlic cloves, thinly sliced

1½ pounds dark leafy greens,
   such as kale or mustard greens,
   stemmed and chopped, still damp
   after washing

Kosher salt and freshly ground black
   pepper

2 cups cooked brown rice (page 46)

PER SERVING: Calories **140**;
Protein **4g**; Carbohydrates **22g**;
Dietary Fiber **3g**; Sugar **2g**;
Total Fat **5g**; Saturated Fat **0g**

With a whole lot more flavor and fiber than your average bowl of white rice, this simple combination of hearty brown rice and garlicky roasted leafy greens is a phenomenal base for revamped beef and broccoli or a wide variety of meals.

1. Preheat the oven to 400°F. Put 2 medium rimmed baking sheets in the oven to heat.

2. In a small sauté pan, heat the oil over medium heat until it begins to shimmer. Add the garlic and cook until soft, about 2 minutes. Remove from the heat and let infuse for 5 minutes.

3. Put the greens in a large bowl, drizzle the garlic and oil over the greens, and, using your hands, rub the oil into the greens so each leaf is lightly coated. Season with salt and pepper.

4. Using potholders, remove the baking sheets from the oven and divide the greens between the pans, making sure the greens are in an even layer. Roast the greens, turning once, until soft and slightly golden brown and charred on the edges, about 10 minutes. Fold the greens into the rice.

SIDES

Broccoli Salad with Anchovy and Vinegar

SERVES 4

4 tablespoons olive oil

3 large garlic cloves, smashed to a paste

4 anchovy fillets, chopped

1 fresno pepper, thinly sliced

3 tablespoons red wine vinegar

1 tablespoon fresh lemon juice

Kosher salt and freshly ground black pepper

1 medium head of broccoli, cut into florets

PER SERVING: Calories **187**; Protein **5g**; Carbohydrates **9g**; Dietary Fiber **5g**; Sugar **3g**; Total Fat **15g**; Saturated Fat **2g**

Maybe it was my childhood dislike of overcooked frozen broccoli; for some reason I do not often use broccoli in my cooking. But I seem to have surrounded myself with broccoli lovers (see Roasted Broccoli with Roasted Lemon and Parmesan, page 204), so I have been eating it more than ever. After all these years, those assistants of mine may have made me a convert! When it comes time for a healthy side dish for your spring holiday or summer barbecue, eschew the oven in favor of a quick blanch and a long soak in this flavor-packed marinade. And I mean loooong—honestly, you want to make this a day before you serve it for maximum flavor; it only gets better and better. This dish is also excellent with broccoli rabe in place of the broccoli.

1. In a small sauté pan, heat the oil over low heat until it begins to shimmer. Add the garlic and anchovies and cook until the garlic is soft and the anchovies have melted into the oil, 3 minutes. Add the fresno pepper and cook for 30 seconds. Remove from the heat, whisk in the vinegar and lemon juice, and season with salt and black pepper. Let sit at room temperature while you blanch the broccoli.

2. Put a few cups of ice cubes in a large bowl and fill three-quarters full with cold water. Bring a large pot of water to a boil and season generously with salt. Add the broccoli and cook for 2 minutes. Drain the broccoli and plunge it into the ice bath until chilled through, about 2 minutes. Drain well and pat dry with paper towels.

3. Put the broccoli in a large bowl, add the dressing, and toss to coat. Season with salt and black pepper. Cover and refrigerate, stirring a few times, for at least 8 hours and up to 24 hours before serving.

Honey-Mustard Glazed Brussels Sprouts

SERVES 6

2 tablespoons Dijon mustard

2 tablespoons honey

Kosher salt and freshly ground black pepper

1¼ pounds medium Brussels sprouts

3 tablespoons olive oil

PER SERVING: Calories **121**; Protein **3g**; Carbohydrates **13g**; Dietary Fiber **3g**; Sugar **7g**; Total Fat **7g**; Saturated Fat **1g**

As little as a decade ago it felt like you couldn't *pay* people to eat Brussels sprouts. I'm happy to say we have moved past the era of overcooked soggy gray mini cabbages, and now, Brussels sprouts, just like kale, have popped up everywhere from fine dining menus to gastropubs. Somewhere along the way, chefs and home cooks learned to roast these delicious little veggies that taste like a cross between a cabbage and broccoli—and America has embraced them.

1. Preheat the oven to 400°F. Put a rimmed baking sheet in the oven for 10 minutes before roasting.

2. In a small bowl, whisk together the mustard and honey and season with salt and pepper.

3. Trim the bottoms of the Brussels sprouts and slice each in half from top to bottom. Put the Brussels sprouts in a large bowl, add the oil and salt and pepper to taste, and toss to coat evenly.

4. Using potholders, carefully remove the baking sheet from the oven and put the Brussels sprouts on the pan, cut side down, in an even layer. Cook, undisturbed, until the sprouts begin to brown on the bottom, about 10 minutes. Turn the sprouts over and continue roasting for 10 minutes.

5. Remove the baking sheet from the oven, add the honey mustard, and carefully toss to coat. Return to the oven and roast until just cooked through, about 5 minutes longer depending on the size of the sprouts.

Roasted Broccoli with Roasted Lemon and Parmesan

SERVES 4

1 large head of broccoli, cut into florets, stem trimmed, peeled, and cut crosswise into 1-inch pieces

2½ tablespoons olive oil

1 large lemon, halved

Kosher salt and freshly ground black pepper

¼ teaspoon red pepper flakes, preferably Calabrian

3 tablespoons freshly grated Parmigiano-Reggiano cheese

PER SERVING: Calories **138**; Protein **6g**; Carbohydrates **8g**; Dietary Fiber **5g**; Sugar **3g**; Total Fat **10g**; Saturated Fat **2g**

My assistants, Stephanie and Sally, make roasted broccoli with lemon and Parmesan for lunch *at least* once a week, every week of the year. Their recipe is based on one from friend and fellow Food Network host Ina Garten, so you know it's good. I'm a fan, too! My spin on the dish includes adding some heat with my favorite Calabrian red pepper flakes and roasting the lemons for extra sweetness. Either way, it is easy, delicious, and so good for you that you will soon be eating it regularly, too. I see a whole lot more vitamin K, vitamin C, folate, and fiber (broccoli is called the healthiest vegetable in the world for a reason) in everyone's future. If you're feeling extra indulgent or fancy, top with Parmesan cheese shavings.

1. Preheat the oven to 400°F.

2. On a rimmed baking sheet, toss the broccoli with 2 tablespoons of the oil and brush the cut sides of the lemon with the remaining ½ tablespoon oil. Season the broccoli liberally with salt and black pepper and sprinkle with the red pepper flakes; spread on the baking sheet in a single layer. Put the lemon halves on each end of the pan, cut side up. Roast, turning once, until the broccoli is crisp-tender and the lemons are soft and golden brown on top, about 20 minutes.

3. Remove the baking sheet from the oven, squeeze the juice from the lemons over the florets, and toss to coat. Sprinkle the cheese over the top and return to the oven for 5 minutes longer. Serve hot or at room temperature.

Roasted Green Beans with Tomatoes and Hazelnuts

SERVES 6

1 pint cherry tomatoes

3 tablespoons olive oil

Kosher salt and freshly ground black pepper

1 pound French green beans, ends trimmed

2 garlic cloves, chopped

2 tablespoons aged sherry vinegar

5 tablespoons coarsely chopped toasted hazelnuts

¼ cup finely chopped fresh flat-leaf parsley

PER SERVING: Calories **142**; Protein **3g**; Carbohydrates **9g**; Dietary Fiber **3g**; Sugar **2g**; Total Fat **11g**; Saturated Fat **1g**

This dish has its roots in two classic side dishes: green beans amandine, which was all the rage in the 1970s, and the southern staple of slow-cooked greens beans and smothered tomatoes. I have borrowed from both and introduced Spain to the mix. I choose to forgo cooking these beans within an inch of their life and keep them green instead of gray by blanching and then roasting them. The tomatoes are quick-roasted instead of slow-cooked, then blended into a garlicky vinaigrette that, complete with sweet, buttery hazelnuts subbing for old-school almonds, coats the beans with rich and bright flavor.

1. Preheat the oven to 425°F.

2. On a rimmed baking sheet, toss the tomatoes with 2 tablespoons of the oil, and season with salt and pepper. Roast until the tomatoes are slightly charred and soft and the juices have evaporated, about 30 minutes.

3. While the tomatoes are roasting, bring a large pot of salted water to a boil. Add the green beans and cook for 1 minute. Drain and immediately rinse with cold water. Transfer to a rimmed baking sheet and pat dry. Toss with the remaining 1 tablespoon oil and season with salt and pepper.

4. Once the tomatoes are done, roast the green beans until slightly golden brown and crisp-tender, 12 minutes.

5. Set aside ¼ cup of the tomatoes. Put the remaining tomatoes in a food processor, add the garlic, vinegar, 3 tablespoons of the nuts, and the parsley, and process until coarsely chopped. Season with salt and pepper. Transfer to plates or a platter, and top with the reserved tomatoes and green beans. Garnish with the remaining 2 tablespoons chopped nuts. Toss before serving.

Marinated Zucchini with Caramelized Onions, Tomatoes, and Herbs

SERVES 4

4 tablespoons extra-virgin olive oil

1 large red onion, thinly sliced

2 garlic cloves, thinly sliced

2 firm medium zucchini, halved lengthwise and sliced crosswise into thin half-moons

Kosher salt and freshly ground black pepper

1 pint grape tomatoes, halved

¼ cup red wine vinegar

2 tablespoons finely chopped fresh flat-leaf parsley

2 tablespoons finely chopped fresh mint

PER SERVING: Calories **189**; Protein **3g**; Carbohydrates **12g**; Dietary Fiber **4g**; Sugar **7g**; Total Fat **15g**; Saturated Fat **2g**

Tender moons of zucchini, tangled with golden onions and garlic, are cooked until just barely warmed through, and then bathed in an herbed vinegar marinade along with sweet grape tomatoes. This summery combination is a perfect example of a healthy, quick, fresh side dish, and the fact that it is best served at room temperature doesn't hurt, either. This is lovely with a piece of sautéed or grilled fish.

1. In a large sauté pan, heat 2 tablespoons of the oil over medium heat until it begins to shimmer. Add the onion and cook until very soft and lightly golden brown, about 15 minutes.

2. Add the garlic and cook for 1 minute. Add the zucchini, season with salt and pepper, and toss to combine. Cook, stirring often, until the zucchini is just heated through and tender, about 5 minutes.

3. Transfer the mixture to a bowl, add the tomatoes, vinegar, parsley, and mint, and season with salt and pepper. Let sit at room temperature for at least 30 minutes and up to 2 hours before serving.

Roasted Spaghetti Squash with Shallot and Herbs

SERVES 4

1 medium-large spaghetti squash

1 tablespoon olive oil

Kosher salt and freshly ground black pepper

2 tablespoons unsalted butter

1 shallot, finely diced

¼ cup chopped fresh dill

¼ cup chopped fresh cilantro

¼ cup chopped fresh chives

½ cup chopped fresh flat-leaf parsley

¼ cup freshly grated Parmigiano-Reggiano cheese

PER SERVING: Calories **165**; Protein **4g**; Carbohydrates **11g**; Dietary Fiber **2g**; Sugar **1g**; Total Fat **12g**; Saturated Fat **5g**

Spaghetti squash gets lots of play as a pasta substitute for the gluten-free, but you should give it a try even if you aren't on a restricted diet. Alive with savory, herbaceous flavor, this makes a great side for any fish or chicken dish or a nice vegetarian entrée with a salad.

1. Preheat the oven to 400°F.

2. With a large, sharp knife, carefully cut the squash in half lengthwise. Scrape out the seeds and stringy flesh with a spoon and discard. Brush the cleaned squash halves with the oil and season with salt and pepper.

3. Put the squash cut side down on a rimmed baking sheet and roast for 45 minutes or until the flesh is tender and the cut side is golden brown (you should be able to pierce the skin with a fork). Remove from the oven and let cool slightly. Using a fork, scrape the squash out of its skin into long, spaghetti-like strands.

4. In a large skillet, melt the butter over medium heat and cook the shallot until soft and beginning to caramelize, being careful not to brown the butter or burn the shallot, about 5 minutes. Reduce the heat to medium-low. Add the reserved spaghetti squash to the pan and toss to combine. Cook until warmed through, 5 minutes, and then remove from the heat.

5. Fold in the herbs and cheese and season with salt and pepper to taste.

Roasted Padrón Peppers

SERVES 4

½ pound padrón peppers

2 tablespoons olive oil

Kosher salt and freshly ground black pepper

Flaky sea salt

PER SERVING: Calories **79**;
Protein **1g**; Carbohydrates **3g**;
Dietary Fiber **1g**; Sugar **0g**;
Total Fat **7g**; Saturated Fat **1g**

Padrón peppers (also called shishito peppers) are small, with an elongated, conical shape and a rich, sweet, and earthy flavor. As for their heat factor, you don't really know until you bite into one! As the saying goes, some are hot and some are not. But don't worry—even the hottest of the bunch will never burn your mouth; rather, they have a nice, slow-building heat. Roasting them brings out a bit of sweetness and intensifies their flavor. Simply seasoned and roasted, these make a good side dish, appetizer, or late-night low-calorie snack.

1. Preheat the oven to 425°F.

2. In a medium bowl, toss the peppers with the oil, kosher salt, and pepper. Spread in an even layer on a rimmed baking sheet. Roast, turning once, until charred on both sides and soft, about 10 minutes.

3. Remove the peppers to a platter and sprinkle with flaky sea salt. Serve hot.

Whole Roasted Cauliflower with Tikka Masala Sauce

SERVES 6

2 tablespoons olive oil

¼ cup finely grated red onion

3 cloves garlic, finely grated or chopped to a paste

2 heaping tablespoons Madras curry powder

Grated zest of 1 lime

Juice of 1 lime

Kosher salt and freshly ground black pepper

1 cup 2% Greek yogurt

1 head of cauliflower, bottom leaves removed and end trimmed

Nonstick cooking spray

Tikka Masala Sauce (recipe follows)

Chopped fresh cilantro or sliced green onion, for garnish (optional)

Lime wedges, for serving

PER SERVING (INCLUDES SAUCE): Calories 209; Protein 7g; Carbohydrates 22g; Dietary Fiber 6g; Sugar 13g; Total Fat 11g; Saturated Fat 2g

The first time I came across a recipe for a whole roasted cauliflower was a few years ago when I was looking for something fun to do as a vegetarian Thanksgiving idea. I decided on something else but have always wanted to revisit it. This Indian-flavored recipe is not only impressive to look at but even more delicious to eat—and healthy, too.

1. In a small nonstick sauté pan, heat the oil over high heat until it begins to shimmer. Add the onion and cook until soft, 2 minutes. Add the garlic and cook for 1 minute longer. Add the curry powder and cook, stirring constantly, until it deepens in color and becomes aromatic, 2 minutes longer. Add 1 cup water and simmer until completely reduced, about 5 minutes. Transfer to a bowl, add the lime zest and juice, and season with 2 teaspoons salt and ¼ teaspoon pepper. Let cool for 5 minutes. Whisk the yogurt into the marinade.

2. Season the entire cauliflower with salt and pepper, rubbing it in. Rub the entire surface with the marinade and let sit at room temperature for at least 30 minutes and up to 1 hour.

3. Preheat the oven to 350°F. Put a cast-iron pan in the oven to heat for 10 minutes.

4. Remove the pan from the oven, spray with nonstick spray, and place the cauliflower in the pan, cut-stem side down. Return to the oven and roast until the cauliflower is golden brown and tender when pierced with a skewer or paring knife, 1½ to 2 hours. Remove from the oven and let the cauliflower rest for 10 minutes before cutting into big florets.

5. Ladle the masala sauce into shallow bowls, and top with cauliflower. Garnish with cilantro or green onion, if desired, and serve with lime wedges.

(Recipe continues)

Tikka Masala Sauce

SERVES 6

2 tablespoons olive oil

1 medium yellow onion, halved and thinly sliced

2-inch piece of fresh ginger, peeled and finely grated

1 serrano pepper, finely diced

3 garlic cloves, finely chopped

1 tablespoon tomato paste

2 teaspoons smoked Spanish paprika

2 teaspoons garam masala

1 (28-ounce) can plum tomatoes and juices, pureed until smooth

¼ to ½ teaspoon chile de árbol or cayenne powder, to taste

1 tablespoon honey

Kosher salt and freshly ground black pepper

¼ cup 2% Greek yogurt

¼ cup chopped fresh cilantro

¼ cup chopped green onion, dark and light green parts

1. In a medium Dutch oven, heat 2 tablespoons of the olive oil over medium heat until it begins to shimmer. Add the onion and cook until soft and lightly golden brown, about 10 minutes.

2. Stir in the ginger, serrano, and garlic and cook for 1 minute. Add the tomato paste, paprika, and garam masala and cook for 1 minute. Add 1 cup water and boil for 5 minutes. Add the tomatoes and chile de árbol and simmer, stirring occasionally, until thickened, about 20 minutes. Stir in the honey and season with salt and black pepper.

3. Remove from the heat and whisk in the yogurt, cilantro, and green onion until combined. Cover and keep warm until serving.

PER SERVING: Calories **101**; Protein **2g**; Carbohydrates **12g**; Dietary Fiber **3g**; Sugar **8g**; Total Fat **5g**; Saturated Fat **1g**

Mustard Greens with Indian Spices

SERVES 4

1 medium red onion, coarsely chopped

3 garlic cloves, chopped

1 to 2 serrano peppers, to taste, chopped

2-inch piece of fresh ginger, peeled and chopped

¼ teaspoon ground turmeric

Kosher salt and freshly ground black pepper

2 tablespoons olive oil

1 pound mustard greens, stemmed, leaves coarsely chopped

1 pound fresh spinach, stemmed, leaves coarsely chopped

PER SERVING: Calories **162**; Protein **6g**; Carbohydrates **20g**; Dietary Fiber **9g**; Sugar **3g**; Total Fat **7g**; Saturated Fat **1g**

This recipe is based on a Northern Indian dish called sarson ka saag that I had recently at a restaurant in New York City. In that instance, the greens were served pureed, almost like a creamed spinach. I prefer to keep the greens coarsely chopped to highlight the different textures of the silky spinach and heartier mustard greens. Totally delicious as a side to grilled meats and fish, the greens can also be spooned onto flatbread, rolled, and eaten as a healthy lunch or afternoon snack.

1. In a food processor, combine the onion, garlic, serrano, ginger, turmeric, and a splash of water and process until smooth. Season with salt and black pepper.

2. In a large high-sided pan, heat the oil over medium heat until it begins to shimmer. Add the onion puree and cook, stirring constantly, until it's fragrant and the color deepens, about 2 minutes.

3. Add the greens, in batches at first if necessary, and cook, adding a few splashes of water if the mixture becomes dry, until the greens are wilted and soft, about 20 minutes. Season with salt and black pepper.

Shredded Veggie Slaw with Celery Seed Vinaigrette

SERVES 6

Spooned atop a turkey sandwich or served aside a burger, coleslaw is a favorite. But most coleslaws contain lots of mayonnaise, which means lots of fat. With all due respect to my favorite delis, it's time for a modern version like this one with crisp veggies and a fresher dressing.

¼ cup apple cider vinegar

2 tablespoons finely grated red or yellow onion

1 tablespoon 2% Greek yogurt

2 teaspoons Dijon mustard

2 heaping teaspoons celery seeds, lightly toasted

1 teaspoon honey

Kosher salt and freshly ground black pepper

¼ cup extra-virgin olive oil

4 cups finely shredded red and green cabbage

2 cups finely shredded kale

1 large carrot, peeled and coarsely shredded

2 green onions, dark and pale green parts, halved lengthwise and thinly sliced crosswise

PER SERVING: Calories **125**; Protein **2g**; Carbohydrates **8g**; Dietary Fiber **2g**; Sugar **4g**; Total Fat **10g**; Saturated Fat **1g**

1. Make the vinaigrette: In a medium bowl, whisk together the vinegar, onion, yogurt, mustard, celery seeds, honey, 1 teaspoon salt, and ¼ teaspoon pepper. Slowly whisk in the olive oil. Let sit for at least 30 minutes to allow the flavors to meld.

2. Combine the cabbage, kale, carrots, and green onions in a large bowl, add the vinaigrette, and season with salt and pepper. Toss well to coat in the dressing. Refrigerate for at least 30 minutes and up to 4 hours before serving.

Steam-Roasted Cauliflower with Honey, Mint, and Currants

SERVES 4

⅓ cup red wine vinegar

2 tablespoons currants

1 heaping tablespoon honey

2 teaspoons capers, drained

2 tablespoons chopped fresh mint

Kosher salt and freshly ground black pepper

1 large head cauliflower, cut into florets

2 tablespoons olive oil

PER SERVING: Calories **137**; Protein **4g**; Carbohydrates **16g**; Dietary Fiber **6g**; Sugar **9g**; Total Fat **7g**; Saturated Fat **1g**

I feel as if cauliflower is finally emerging from its evil-stepsister-of-the-veggie-world status. I have always served it in my restaurants, in soups, purees, even fried, and it's on my must-order list whenever I see it on other menus. This steam-roast hybrid method helps cook the cauliflower through before it gets too much color or burns on the outside. The cauliflower still gets all the rich roasted flavor from the oven's high heat, but the water keeps it light. With all of its bright, sweet-and-salty flavors, this dish has become one the most popular offerings at my restaurant Gato in New York City.

1. Preheat the oven to 400°F. Put a rimmed baking sheet in the oven 10 minutes before cooking the cauliflower.

2. Pour the vinegar into a small nonreactive saucepan, bring to a simmer, and add the currants and honey. Remove from the heat and let cool to room temperature. Stir in the capers and mint and season with salt and pepper.

3. Put the cauliflower in a bowl, add the oil, and season with salt and pepper. Toss to combine. Using oven mitts, carefully remove the baking sheet. Arrange the cauliflower in a single layer on the pan, add ½ cup water, and immediately return to the oven. Cook, turning once, until the florets are just cooked through, about 15 minutes.

4. Remove to a platter and drizzle with the dressing. Let sit at room temperature for at least 30 minutes and up to 2 hours to allow the flavors to meld before serving.

Roasted Carrots with Spanish Spices and Harissa Yogurt Sauce

SERVES 4

½ cup 2% Greek yogurt

1 tablespoon harissa

1 tablespoon finely chopped fresh flat-leaf parsley, plus whole leaves for garnish

1 teaspoon finely chopped fresh thyme, plus whole sprigs for garnish

1 teaspoon finely grated lemon zest

Kosher salt and freshly ground black pepper

1 pound baby carrots, tops removed but with a little green left attached (use real baby carrots, not the large carrots that have been whittled down)

3 tablespoons olive oil

2 teaspoons Spanish paprika

½ teaspoon ground cumin

½ teaspoon ground mustard

¼ teaspoon ground fennel

2 teaspoons light brown sugar

PER SERVING: Calories **165**; Protein **3g**; Carbohydrates **12g**; Dietary Fiber **2g**; Sugar **8g**; Total Fat **12g**; Saturated Fat **2g**

This vegetable side dish has been on my menu at Gato since it opened and continues to be one of the best-selling items at the restaurant. These carrots are rubbed with spices and cooked just until crisp-tender. Carrots are the source not only of beta-carotene, but also of a wide variety of antioxidants and other health-supporting nutrients.

1. In a medium bowl, whisk together the yogurt, harissa, parsley, thyme, and lemon zest and season with salt and pepper. Cover and let the flavors meld while you prepare the carrots.

2. Bring a pot of well-salted water to a boil. Set up a bowl of well-salted ice water. Blanch the carrots in the boiling water until crisp-tender, about 5 minutes. Scoop them out and plunge them immediately into the ice water for 2 minutes to cool. Drain well. Use a clean kitchen towel to rub the skin off the carrots (instead of peeling them first; this is super simple).

3. In a heavy skillet, preferably cast iron, heat the oil over medium heat until it shimmers. Add the carrots, paprika, cumin, mustard, fennel, and brown sugar and cook until the carrots are charred. Season with salt and pepper. Transfer the carrots to a platter and top with dollops of the yogurt sauce.

Roasted Radishes with Fines Herbes

SERVES 4

1 pound radishes, stems mostly removed, halved lengthwise

3 tablespoons extra-virgin olive oil

Kosher salt and freshly ground black pepper

1 tablespoon finely chopped fresh flat-leaf parsley

1 tablespoon finely chopped fresh chives

1 tablespoon finely chopped fresh tarragon

PER SERVING: Calories **116**; Protein **1g**; Carbohydrates **4g**; Dietary Fiber **2g**; Sugar **2g**; Total Fat **11g**; Saturated Fat **2g**

People love radishes sliced in salads, served with butter and salt on a baguette, and garnishing a Bloody Mary, but how about roasted? You can go ahead and add the radish to the list of things you never thought to cook (romaine lettuce, this one is looking at you!) but should. Peppery, crunchy radishes become sweet and tender after a stint in the oven. They're wonderful as a side dish (try topping with Salsa Verde, page 151), alongside grilled meat or fish, or on top of yogurt for a savory way to start your day.

1. Preheat the oven to 400°F.

2. On a rimmed baking sheet, toss the radishes in 2 tablespoons of the oil and season with salt and pepper. Roast, turning once, until slightly caramelized and soft, about 30 minutes.

3. Remove from the oven and transfer to a platter or bowl. Sprinkle the herbs over the radishes and drizzle with the remaining 1 tablespoon oil; season with salt to taste. Serve hot or at room temperature.

White Bean Colcannon

SERVES 4

2 slices bacon, cut into ½-inch dice

4 tablespoons extra-virgin olive oil

2 garlic cloves, thinly sliced

1 teaspoon mustard seeds

⅛ teaspoon red pepper flakes, preferably Calabrian

1 pound coarsely chopped mustard greens, collard greens, or kale (or a combination), stemmed and slightly damp

Kosher salt and freshly ground black pepper

1 teaspoon sugar

2 tablespoons apple cider vinegar

8 ounces dried white beans, cooked (see page 47) with onion, garlic, and thyme, 2 cups of the cooking liquid reserved, warm

2 green onions, dark green and pale green parts, thinly sliced

PER SERVING: Calories **401**; Protein **17g**; Carbohydrates **42g**; Dietary Fiber **12g**; Sugar **9g**; Total Fat **19g**; Saturated Fat **4g**

The Irish prepare this dish with potatoes and lots of bacon, cream, and butter. Delicious? Absolutely. Good for you? Not so much. But in an effort to embrace this ancestral dish (that's right, I'm Irish!), I'm all about this white bean–based version. It has a lot more fiber and protein than the original and quite a bit less fat. There's no real need for all the cream and butter—whipped-up white beans are naturally creamy. I use a small amount of bacon (pork or turkey) for its rich smokiness, but you can leave it out if you'd rather keep this vegetarian. Just a note: Most of my recipes that call for beans allow you to substitute canned, but this isn't one of them. You definitely want to make this with dried beans, keeping some of the cooking liquid for use in one of the later steps.

1. Put a large sauté pan over medium heat and add the bacon. Cook, stirring occasionally, until the fat is rendered and the bacon is crisp, about 8 minutes. Remove the bacon with a slotted spoon to a plate lined with paper towels. Discard all but 1 tablespoon of the bacon fat from the pan.

2. Add the olive oil to the pan and heat over medium heat until the oil begins to shimmer. Add the garlic, mustard seeds, and red pepper flakes and cook for 1 minute. Increase the heat to high, add the greens, in batches if needed, season with salt and black pepper, and cook, tossing constantly at first, until the greens begin to wilt, about 2 minutes. Continue cooking, stirring occasionally, until crisp-tender, about 8 minutes. Add the sugar and vinegar and cook for 2 minutes longer.

3. Transfer the beans to a food processor and process until coarsely ground. Begin adding the cooking liquid, ¼ cup at a time, and process until smooth and creamy, adding more liquid if needed. Season with salt and black pepper.

4. Scrape the bean mixture into a bowl and fold in the mustard greens and green onion. Top with the bacon.

Grilled Radicchio and Kale Sauerkraut Style

SERVES 8

Don't knock it till you try it: grilled radicchio and kale are terrific, their appealing bitterness at once highlighted and tamed by the smoky flames. This sweet and acidic dressing takes its inspiration from sauerkraut and combines with the grilled lettuces to make a great summer side dish. Just like its fermented counterpart, this goes well with chicken, steak, lean sausages, and pork.

½ cup plus 3 tablespoons canola oil

1 small shallot, chopped

½ cup apple cider vinegar

1 tablespoon sugar

8 juniper berries

½ teaspoon caraway seeds

½ teaspoon yellow mustard seeds

3 fresh thyme sprigs

Kosher salt and freshly ground black pepper

3 heads of radicchio, halved

2 big bunches of dinosaur (lacinato) kale, soaked in cold water

PER SERVING: Calories **218**; Protein **2g**; Carbohydrates **8g**; Dietary Fiber **1g**; Sugar **3g**; Total Fat **20g**; Saturated Fat **2g**

1. In a small saucepan, heat 1 tablespoon of the oil over medium heat. Add the shallot and cook until soft, about 2 minutes. Add the vinegar, sugar, juniper berries, caraway, mustard seeds, thyme, 1 teaspoon salt, and ¼ teaspoon pepper. Bring to a boil and cook until the sugar and salt are dissolved, 1 minute. Remove from the heat and let macerate for 30 minutes and up to 2 hours at room temperature. Strain into a small bowl, discarding the solids. Slowly whisk in ½ cup of the oil until emulsified.

2. Heat a grill to high or a grill pan over high heat.

3. Brush the cut side of the radicchio heads with 1 tablespoon of the oil and season with salt and pepper. Grill, cut side down, until golden brown and slightly charred, 2 to 3 minutes. Brush the tops with the remaining 1 tablespoon oil, flip over, and continue grilling until just heated through, 2 to 3 minutes longer. Transfer to a cutting board, thinly slice the radicchio, and put in a large bowl.

4. Remove the bunches of kale from the water and shake gently. Season with salt and pepper and put on the grill (wet so it can steam a little). Grill until slightly wilted and charred on all sides, about 1 minute per side. Remove, thinly slice, and add to the radicchio.

5. Add the dressing to the salad and toss to coat. Let sit at room temperature for 30 minutes to allow the flavors to meld before serving.

Spicy Maple-Roasted Hasselback Sweet Potatoes

SERVES 4

4 medium sweet potatoes, scrubbed

4 tablespoons (½ stick) unsalted butter

¼ cup pure maple syrup

2 teaspoons canned chipotle in adobo

Pinch of kosher salt

PER SERVING: Calories **319**; Protein **2g**; Carbohydrates **41g**; Dietary Fiber **4g**; Sugar **24g**; Total Fat **17g**; Saturated Fat **7g**

I love sweet potatoes. Low in calories and high in beta-carotene, these healthy tubers shouldn't be reserved just for Thanksgiving. I use them year-round in soups, desserts, and side dishes, including this standout. Showcasing some easy knife work, not only do they look impressive on the table, but the sweet, smoky glaze also adds a bit of a crispy texture to the outside of the skin.

1. Preheat the oven to 425°F.

2. Rinse and dry the potatoes. Then using a sharp knife, cut slices about ½ inch thick, two thirds of the way through the potatoes. Put the potatoes on a rimmed baking sheet lined with parchment paper. Roast for 45 minutes.

3. In a small saucepan, melt the butter over low heat, add the maple syrup and chipotle, and season with salt. Keep warm.

4. Brush each potato with the glaze and return to the oven to continue roasting until the flesh is cooked through and the skin is crisp, about 10 minutes longer.

Salt-Roasted Potatoes

SERVES 6

1¼ pounds small new Yukon Gold or red potatoes

2½ cups coarse sea salt or kosher salt

2 teaspoons whole black peppercorns

2 tablespoons coarsely chopped fresh tarragon

2 tablespoons chopped fresh thyme

2 tablespoons chopped fresh rosemary

Coarsely grated zest of 1 orange

1 head of garlic, halved crosswise

PER SERVING: Calories **68**; Protein **2g**; Carbohydrates **15g**; Dietary Fiber **2g**; Sugar **1g**; Total Fat **0g**; Saturated Fat **0g**

Roasting new potatoes with flavored salt is a fantastic way to infuse the potatoes with depth and get a buttery, creamy interior texture with a crisp exterior, without all the fat of french fries.

1. Preheat the oven to 400°F.

2. Prick the potatoes a few times with a fork. Put the potatoes in a large roasting pan. In a small bowl, combine the salt, peppercorns, tarragon, thyme, rosemary, and orange zest, and sprinkle the mixture evenly over the potatoes. Set the garlic halves among the potatoes.

3. Cover the dish with foil and roast the potatoes for 15 minutes. Remove the foil and continue roasting until the potatoes are light golden brown and just cooked through, about 20 minutes longer. Carefully remove the potatoes from the pan, wiping off any excess salt.

VARIATION

Lemon-Sage–Roasted Potatoes

Replace the tarragon, thyme, rosemary, and orange zest with 3 tablespoons chopped fresh sage and the grated the zest of 2 lemons.

Roasted Cabbage Steaks with Caraway Vinaigrette

SERVES 6

1 teaspoon caraway seeds

¼ cup aged sherry vinegar

1 heaping tablespoon Dijon mustard

1 teaspoon finely chopped fresh thyme

Kosher salt and freshly ground black pepper

½ cup extra-virgin olive oil

1 small head of red cabbage, tough outer leaves removed, sliced into 1-inch-thick rounds (3 rounds)

1 small head of green cabbage, tough outer leaves removed, sliced into 1-inch-thick rounds (3 rounds)

PER SERVING: Calories **249**; Protein **3g**; Carbohydrates **17g**; Dietary Fiber **6g**; Sugar **10g**; Total Fat **20g**; Saturated Fat **3g**

I'll admit it, the first time I saw "cauliflower steak" on a menu, I was confused—a steak topped with cauliflower? Now that I'm familiar with the "steak" referring to the center cut of the vegetable, left whole and cooked as a beef steak would be, I'm ready to give the steak treatment to another species from the garden: cabbage. If you're on the fence about cabbage, try this dish and see; you'll be on the magnesium-, calcium-, vitamin-, and fiber-rich bandwagon after a single bite.

1. In a small sauté pan, toast the caraway seeds over low heat until just fragrant. Transfer to a cutting board and lightly crush with the bottom of a cool pan.

2. In a small bowl, whisk together the vinegar, mustard, and thyme and season with salt and pepper. Slowly whisk in ¼ cup oil until emulsified and then stir in the caraway seeds. Let sit at room temperature while you prepare the cabbage.

3. Preheat the oven to 400°F.

4. Line a rimmed baking sheet with parchment paper. Put the cabbage on the baking sheet, brush both sides of the cabbage with the remaining ¼ cup oil, and season with salt and pepper. Roast the cabbage until soft and lightly golden brown, about 25 minutes. Remove to a platter and immediately spoon the vinaigrette over the top.

Parsnips and Carrots en Papillote with Wine, Maple, and Thyme

SERVES 6

¾ pounds carrots, peeled and cut into thick batons

¾ pounds parsnips, peeled and cut into thick batons

2 tablespoons olive oil

1 tablespoon melted unsalted butter

1 tablespoon pure maple syrup

1 tablespoon finely chopped fresh thyme, plus more for garnish

Splash of dry white wine

Kosher salt and freshly ground black pepper

PER SERVING: Calories **126**; Protein **1g**; Carbohydrates **16g**; Dietary Fiber **4g**; Sugar **8g**; Total Fat **7g**; Saturated Fat **2g**

Sealing ingredients inside a tidy parchment packet is an excellent way to cook with very little to no fat yet still achieve perfect texture and tons of flavor. Fish *en papillote* was one of my favorite dishes I learned in culinary school, and I love the technique just as much for cooking root vegetables. They emerge lightly caramelized and still slightly al dente. I like the contrasting colors and flavors of carrots and parsnips together—the parsnip may look like an ivory carrot, but its earthy and nutty flavor is so much more.

1. Preheat the oven to 425°F. Line a rimmed baking sheet with parchment paper.

2. Put the carrots and parsnips in a large bowl, add the oil, butter, maple syrup, thyme, and wine, and season with salt and pepper. Loosely mound the vegetables in the center of the parchment paper on the baking sheet. Fold the parchment up over the vegetables in the center and at the edges, sealing it well so steam won't escape.

3. Bake until the veggies are crisp-tender, about 30 minutes. Transfer the packet to a platter and carefully cut it open (hot steam will escape). Sprinkle additional fresh thyme on top, if desired, and serve.

Roasted Peppers with Garlicky Bread Crumbs

SERVES 6

4 tablespoons olive oil

3 garlic cloves, smashed to a paste

2 anchovy fillets, chopped

½ cup fresh whole-wheat bread crumbs

Kosher salt and freshly ground black pepper

3 red bell peppers, stems removed

3 yellow bell peppers, stems removed

3 orange bell peppers, stems removed

2 tablespoons extra-virgin olive oil

A few dashes of red wine vinegar (optional)

8 fresh basil leaves, torn

PER SERVING: Calories **213**; Protein **3g**; Carbohydrates **18g**; Dietary Fiber **3g**; Sugar **5g**; Total Fat **15g**; Saturated Fat **2g**

Mediterranean cuisines are all known for their mezze— appetizers or small plates meant for sharing. In Italy, that spread will always include some kind of roasted peppers. This is my version. Great as an appetizer, the sweet peppers with their crisp, savory crumb topping are also excellent served on top of simply prepared chicken or fish.

1. In a small nonstick sauté pan, heat 2 tablespoons of the olive oil over medium heat until it begins to shimmer. Add the garlic and cook until soft, about 1 minute. Add the anchovies and cook for 30 seconds longer.

2. Add the bread crumbs, season with salt and pepper, and cook, stirring constantly, until golden brown and crisp, about 7 minutes.

3. Preheat the oven to 425°F.

4. Rub the peppers with the remaining 2 tablespoons olive oil and season with salt and pepper. Transfer to a baking sheet and roast in the oven until soft and blistered on all sides, turning every 5 minutes, about 20 minutes. Remove the peppers to a large bowl, cover with plastic wrap, and let steam for 15 minutes.

5. Remove the skin and seeds from the peppers and discard. Slice the flesh into 1-inch-thick slices. Transfer to a platter, drizzle with the 2 tablespoons extra-virgin olive oil and the vinegar, if using, and scatter the basil on top. Let sit at room temperature for 30 minutes. Top with the bread crumbs just before serving.

Spinach and Tomato Quinoa

SERVES 6

3 tablespoons olive oil

1 large Spanish onion, halved and thinly sliced

1 garlic clove, finely chopped

2 tablespoons tomato paste

1½ pounds fresh spinach, stemmed, leaves coarsely chopped

2 cups Best Vegetable Stock (page 140) or low-sodium store-bought stock, or water

1 cup quinoa

Kosher salt and freshly ground black pepper

¼ cup chopped fresh dill

1 cup grape tomatoes, halved

1 lemon, cut in wedges

PER SERVING: Calories **222**; Protein **7g**; Carbohydrates **30g**; Dietary Fiber **5g**; Sugar **6g**; Total Fat **9g**; Saturated Fat **1g**

Time and again, I look to the deliciously healthy food of Greece when I need sustenance and inspiration. This particular dish has its roots in spanakorizo, a Greek spinach dish typically made with white rice. Using quinoa adds a texture that I love, as well as protein and fiber. Serve this with chicken, pork, or fish or add protein-packed chickpeas for an easy vegetarian entrée.

1. In a large high-sided sauté pan, heat the oil over medium heat until it begins to shimmer. Add the onion and cook until very soft and pale beige, about 8 minutes. Add the garlic and cook for 30 seconds. Stir in the tomato paste and cook for 1 minute longer. Add the spinach and stir until just wilted.

2. Pour the stock into the pan, and bring to a boil. Add the quinoa, season with salt and pepper, and cook until the liquid is absorbed, about 20 minutes. Remove from the heat and let sit covered for 5 minutes.

3. Stir in the dill and tomatoes and transfer to a bowl. Squeeze the lemon over the top before serving.

DESSERTS

Almond Granita with Sour Cherry Compote

SERVES 6

Almond Granita

2 cups almond milk

½ cup lightly toasted slivered almonds

¼ cup sugar

Scant ¼ cup canned almond paste

1 teaspoon finely grated orange zest

½ teaspoon pure almond extract

Sour Cherry Compote

¼ cup sugar

Juice of 1 small lemon

2½ cups (1 pound) fresh or frozen sour cherries, pitted

1 tablespoon kirsch (optional)

1 teaspoon pure vanilla extract

PER SERVING: Calories **215**; Protein **4g**; Carbohydrates **31g**; Dietary Fiber **3g**; Sugar **24g**; Total Fat **9g**; Saturated Fat **1g**

This icy granita made with almond milk is lighter in calories and fat than ice cream while still rich and satisfying in flavor. Almonds and cherries are one of my favorite flavor pairings, and I love serving the ice-cold granita with the tart cherry compote while the latter is still slightly warm: The contrast of textures and temperatures makes for a really wonderful and satisfying dessert. If you can't find sour cherries, dark cherries will work as well.

1. Make the almond granita: In a blender, combine the almond milk with ¼ cup of the slivered almonds, the sugar, almond paste, orange zest, and almond extract and puree until smooth. Pour the mixture into a 9 × 9-inch baking dish, cover the dish with plastic wrap, and put in the freezer.

2. Using the tines of a fork, stir the mixture every 30 minutes, scraping the edges and breaking up any ice chunks as the mixture freezes, until the granita is slushy and frozen, about 3 hours.

3. Make the cherry compote: In a heavy medium saucepan, combine 1 cup water with the sugar and lemon juice. Bring to a boil over high heat, stir, and cook until the sugar dissolves and the mixture is reduced by half.

4. Stir in the cherries, reduce the heat to medium, and cook until the cherries are slightly softened but still retain some of their shape, about 5 minutes. Remove from the heat, stir in the kirsch, if using, and the vanilla, and let cool for at least 5 minutes. The compote can be cooled completely, covered, and refrigerated for up to a week.

5. Scoop the granita into chilled serving glasses or bowls and top with the sour cherry compote and remaining ¼ cup almonds.

Coffee-Caramel Yogurt Panna Cotta

SERVES 6

Coffee Caramel

1 cup strongly brewed coffee

⅓ cup sugar

½ teaspoon pure vanilla extract

Nonstick cooking spray

Panna Cotta

2 cups low-fat (1%) milk

1 packet (2¼ teaspoons) unflavored gelatin

¼ cup sugar

1⅔ cups 2% Greek yogurt

1 teaspoon pure vanilla extract

1 ounce bittersweet chocolate, finely chopped

PER SERVING: Calories **182**; Protein **7g**; Carbohydrates **30g**; Dietary Fiber **0g**; Sugar **28g**; Total Fat **4g**; Saturated Fat **2g**

This chocolate-flecked flan-like dessert has that same crowning layer of sweet caramel (emboldened here by coffee) dripping over every bite as does the traditional one adored across Spain and Latin America. But what it doesn't have is eggs. Instead, the custard gets its stability from gelatin, much like an Italian panna cotta. Making it lighter still is creamy Greek yogurt, the perfect swap for caloric cream.

1. Make the coffee caramel: In a saucepan, bring the coffee and sugar to a boil over high heat. Cook until thickened and reduced to about ½ cup. Remove from the heat and stir in the vanilla. Let cool to room temperature (it will thicken).

2. Spray six 6-ounce ramekins with nonstick spray. Spoon a heaping tablespoon of coffee caramel into each ramekin.

3. Make the panna cotta: Pour ½ cup milk into a small bowl, sprinkle the gelatin on top, and let stand for 1 minute. Stir and let stand 10 minutes longer to allow the gelatin to soften.

4. In a small saucepan, combine the remaining 1½ cups milk and the sugar, bring to a boil over high heat, and cook, stirring, until the sugar has dissolved, about 1 minute. Add the softened gelatin mixture and whisk gently until dissolved and smooth, about 2 minutes. Remove from the heat and let cool until lukewarm.

5. In a medium bowl, whisk together the yogurt and vanilla, add the cooled milk mixture, and gently whisk until combined. Strain the mixture through a mesh strainer into a pitcher and stir in the chocolate. Divide the mixture among the ramekins, cover, and refrigerate for at least 4 hours and up to 24 hours before serving.

6. To serve, fill a small bowl halfway with very hot water. Run a small metal spatula between the panna cottas and sides of the ramekins to loosen. Invert a small plate atop a ramekin, hold the plate and ramekin together, and turn upside down, giving a firm shake to release and easing out the panna cotta with a spatula if needed. Dip the ramekin into the hot water to dissolve any of the caramel left in the bottom of the ramekin and pour over the panna cotta. Repeat with the remaining panna cottas.

Banana Split with Spiced Strawberries and Pistachios

SERVES 4

¼ cup unsweetened flaked coconut

1 (14-ounce) can full-fat coconut milk, refrigerated for 24 hours

2 tablespoons agave syrup or honey

1 teaspoon pure vanilla extract

4 firm ripe bananas, peeled and halved lengthwise

½ small pineapple, peeled, cored, and diced

Spiced Strawberries (recipe follows)

¼ cup cocoa nibs (optional)

¼ cup roasted pistachios, chopped

PER SERVING (INCLUDES STRAWBERRIES): Calories **473**; Protein **8g**; Carbohydrates **67g**; Dietary Fiber **8g**; Sugar **54g**; Total Fat **21g**; Saturated Fat **17g**

One thing I am often asked is what I would choose for my last meal on Earth, and my answer always concludes with ice cream, specifically a banana split. But when you know that it's not your last meal, and when in fact your aim is to be around for as many meals as you can, make this instead. Whipping coconut milk creates the most amazing creamy texture. Every berry-loaded bite of this is a treat.

1. Preheat the oven to 325°F.

2. Spread the coconut on a rimmed baking sheet and toast, turning once, until lightly golden brown and crispy, about 10 minutes. Set aside to cool.

3. Ten minutes before you are ready to whip the coconut cream, put the mixing bowl and whisk attachment in the freezer to chill.

4. Remove the can of coconut milk from the refrigerator without shaking or tipping it. Remove the lid of the can and carefully, using a spoon, scoop the thick layer of coconut cream from the top and transfer it to the chilled mixing bowl. (Reserve the coconut water that has settled to the bottom of the can for another use.)

5. Whip the cream on medium speed until light and fluffy. Add the agave syrup and vanilla and continue to whip until incorporated. Fold in half of the toasted coconut, cover, and chill until ready to serve.

6. To serve, put 2 banana halves and some pineapple on a plate. Top with a dollop of the coconut whipped cream, drizzle with the strawberries, and garnish with cocoa nibs, if using, pistachios, and the remaining toasted coconut.

Spiced Strawberries

SERVES 4

1 quart strawberries, halved if small, quartered if large

1 teaspoon finely grated orange zest

Juice of ½ orange

1 tablespoon honey

½ vanilla bean, split lengthwise, seeds scraped

2 cardamom pods, lightly crushed

1 star anise

2 cinnamon sticks

In a medium bowl, combine the strawberries, orange zest and juice, and honey and let sit for 5 minutes. Coarsely smash the berries (leaving some texture) and add the vanilla bean and seeds, cardamom pods, star anise, and cinnamon stick. Cover and let macerate in the refrigerator, mixing a few times, for at least 4 hours and up to 24 hours. Discard the vanilla bean pod and spices before serving.

PER SERVING: Calories **72**; Protein **1g**; Carbohydrates **16g**; Dietary Fiber **4g**; Sugar **12g**; Total Fat **1g**; Saturated Fat **0g**

Bittersweet Maple Bark with Quinoa, Cashews, Apricots, and Cherries

MAKES 12 PIECES

3 tablespoons pure maple syrup

1 tablespoon coconut oil, melted, or extra-virgin olive oil

½ teaspoon pure vanilla extract

1 teaspoon finely grated orange zest

⅛ teaspoon fine sea salt

⅓ cup (uncooked) quinoa

¾ cup coarsely chopped almonds

¾ cup coarsely chopped cashews

8 ounces bittersweet chocolate, at least 71% cacao, coarsely chopped

1 teaspoon instant espresso powder

¼ cup finely diced dried apricots

¼ cup chopped unsweetened dried cherries

PER PIECE: Calories **256**; Protein **5g**; Carbohydrates **27g**; Dietary Fiber **3g**; Sugar **15g**; Total Fat **15g**; Saturated Fat **6g**

The first thing I look for when I walk into a chocolate store is almond bark with dried fruit. Truth be told, I usually go for the milk chocolate version because, like most Americans of my generation, that's what I grew up eating. But the more that I travel and the older I get, the more I've come to appreciate a really great piece of dark chocolate—and it doesn't hurt to read that a piece of bittersweet chocolate (that is at least 71% cacao) a day is actually good for you. Also on the good-for-you ingredient list: everyone's favorite, quinoa. I love the crispy taste—think grown-up Rice Krispies!

1. Preheat the oven to 325°F. Line a rimmed baking sheet with a silicone baking mat or parchment paper.

2. In a medium bowl, whisk together the maple syrup, oil, vanilla, orange zest, and salt and fold in the quinoa and nuts. Spread the mixture onto the prepared baking sheet into an even 9-inch square. Bake until the quinoa and nuts are lightly golden brown and the mixture is crisp, about 25 minutes. Remove to a rack and let cool.

3. Put a few inches of water in a medium saucepan and bring to a simmer over low heat. Put the chocolate and espresso powder in a heat-proof metal bowl and set the bowl on top of the saucepan, making sure that the water doesn't touch the bowl. Slowly heat, stirring, until the chocolate is smooth and shiny and just melted.

4. Remove from the heat and evenly spread the chocolate over the top of the quinoa crunch. Scatter the apricots and cherries over the top and refrigerate until set, about 20 minutes. Cut or break into 12 equal pieces. Store covered in a container for up to 1 week in the refrigerator.

Deconstructed Mulled Wine–Poached Pear Crisp

SERVES 8

Crisp

½ cup all-purpose flour

½ cup whole-wheat flour

1 teaspoon baking powder

3 tablespoons granulated sugar

3 tablespoons Demerara or turbinado sugar (such as Sugar in the Raw)

10 tablespoons (1¼ sticks) unsalted butter, melted

Poached Pears

1 (750-ml) bottle good red wine, such as Merlot, Pinot Noir, or Cabernet Sauvignon

½ cup granulated sugar

8 whole cloves

3 star anise

3 cinnamon sticks

¼ teaspoon freshly grated nutmeg

1 vanilla bean, split lengthwise, seeds scraped

2 (3-inch-long) strips of orange zest

Juice of 1 orange

Juice of ½ lemon

4 slightly ripe Bosc or Anjou pears, peeled, halved, and cored

Honey-Vanilla Yogurt (recipe follows)

PER SERVING (INCLUDES YOGURT): Calories **355**; Protein **4g**; Carbohydrates **49g**; Dietary Fiber **2g**; Sugar **33g**; Total Fat **15g**; Saturated Fat **9g**

Poaching fruit in wine is such an elegant, light way to end a meal, and—music to my ears—it couldn't be simpler. A bit of baking is involved in this recipe, but the crunchy crisp garnish is more than worth the minimal effort. Antioxidant-rich red wine, laden with spices, infuses the pears with gorgeous color and complex flavor as they cook, and is later reduced to a glossy syrup to finish the dish in style.

1. Make the crisp: Preheat the oven to 350°F.

2. In a mixing bowl, combine the flours, baking powder, sugars, and butter. Mix until small and large clumps form. Refrigerate until just chilled, 15 minutes.

3. Spread the mixture in an even layer on a rimmed baking sheet and bake until lightly golden brown, about 20 minutes. Remove to a baking rack to cool; as the crisp cools it will get even crunchier.

4. Poach the pears: In a medium nonreactive high-sided sauté pan, combine the wine, sugar, cloves, star anise, cinnamon, nutmeg, vanilla bean and seeds, orange zest and juice, and lemon juice. Bring the mixture to a boil and cook until the sugar has dissolved, about 5 minutes. Reduce the heat to medium and let the mixture simmer.

5. Carefully add the pears to the wine mixture, cut side down, and bring to a simmer. Lower the heat so that the wine continues to simmer gently and poach the pears, turning them once halfway through, until a paring knife or skewer inserted into the center of the pear meets with no resistance, about 20 minutes. Remove the pan from the heat and let the pears sit in the poaching liquid for 15 minutes. Remove the pears to a plate and cover loosely with plastic wrap.

6. Return the poaching liquid to the stove and cook over high heat, stirring occasionally, until reduced to about 1½ cups, about 30 minutes. Strain the liquid through a strainer into a bowl or pitcher and let cool for 10 minutes.

7. Serve topped with some of the crisp, and drizzled with some of the mulled wine syrup and a dollop of the yogurt.

Honey-Vanilla Yogurt

MAKES 1 CUP

1 cup 2% Greek yogurt

2 tablespoons skim milk

1 tablespoon honey

¼ teaspoon pure vanilla extract

In a medium bowl, whisk together the yogurt, milk, honey, and vanilla until combined. Cover and refrigerate for at least 30 minutes and up to 24 hours to allow the flavors to meld.

PER 2 TABLESPOONS: Calories **29**; Protein **2g**; Carbohydrates **4g**; Dietary Fiber **0g**; Sugar **4g**; Total Fat **1g**; Saturated Fat **0g**

Individual New York–Style Strawberry Cheesecake

SERVES 1

Cheesecake

1 (7-ounce) container 2% Greek yogurt

1 tablespoon sugar

1 teaspoon finely grated lemon zest

1 teaspoon pure vanilla extract

Pinch of kosher salt

1 graham cracker, finely crushed

Strawberries

6 large strawberries, finely diced

1 tablespoon sugar

1 tablespoon fresh lemon juice

Grated orange zest, for garnish

PER SERVING: Calories **306**; Protein **14g**; Carbohydrates **49g**; Dietary Fiber **3g**; Sugar **41g**; Total Fat **5g**; Saturated Fat **3g**

I promise you, this Greek yogurt–based cheesecake is every bit as rich and creamy as a New York cheesecake, but it has virtually none of the fat and a tenth of the calories. It's delicious, so easy, and something you'll thank me for on a sweltering summer day because it's totally no-bake. Someone has to say it: This recipe is GENIUS. I call for strawberries since they feel like the classic cheesecake accompaniment, but of course feel free to use blueberries, raspberries, or any ripe fruit that you love. You can make as many or as few of these as you like; the recipe doubles and quadruples easily.

1. Make the cheesecake: In a medium bowl, whisk together the yogurt, sugar, lemon zest, vanilla, and salt. Line a mesh strainer with 2 sheets of cheesecloth (make sure there is at least a 4-inch overhang). Scrape the mixture into the strainer and press down to mold it into the round shape of the strainer. Put the strainer over a bowl and refrigerate for at least 8 hours and up to 24 hours.

2. Marinate the strawberries: In a small bowl, combine the strawberries, sugar, and lemon juice. Cover and refrigerate for at least 30 minutes and up to 1 hour.

3. Remove the cheesecake from the refrigerator and open up the cheesecloth. Sprinkle the graham cracker crumbs over the top of the cheesecake, pressing them in gently to adhere (this will become the bottom). Put a dessert plate on top and invert the cheesecake onto the plate. Top with the strawberries and garnish with orange zest.

Olive Oil Brownies with Toasted Bread Crumbs

MAKES 12 BROWNIES

Brownies

Nonstick cooking spray

2 tablespoons unsalted butter, cut into cubes

3 ounces high-quality unsweetened chocolate, coarsely chopped

2 ounces high-quality bittersweet chocolate, coarsely chopped

½ teaspoon espresso powder

2 large eggs

½ cup granulated sugar

¼ cup packed light brown muscovado sugar

½ cup plus 2 tablespoons mild extra-virgin olive oil, such as Sistema Organa

1 teaspoon pure vanilla extract

Pinch of fine sea salt

½ cup unbleached all-purpose flour

2 ounces coarsely chopped semisweet chocolate

Glaze

½ cup bittersweet chocolate chips

2 teaspoons mild extra-virgin olive oil

Olive Oil–Toasted Bread Crumbs (recipe follows)

PER SERVING (INCLUDES BREAD CRUMBS): Calories **384**; Protein **4g**; Carbohydrates **33g**; Dietary Fiber **2g**; Sugar **17g**; Total Fat **27g**; Saturated Fat **9g**

Baking with olive oil may seem strange to Americans, but Mediterranean cooks have been doing it for centuries with great results! Olive oil gives baked goods, such as cakes, cookies, quick breads, and muffins, a lovely fruity, floral flavor as well as a light texture. More important, olive oil is a healthy fat choice that cuts back the cholesterol and saturated-fat content of desserts. But rest assured that these are still brownies, and richly flavored ones at that; a small square with a cup of espresso is all you need to satisfy a sweet tooth.

1. Make the brownies: Put a rack in the middle of the oven and preheat the oven to 325°F. Spray an 8-inch square baking pan with nonstick spray. Line with foil, leaving an overhang on two opposite sides. Spray the foil.

2. In a medium, heat-proof bowl set over a pan of simmering water, combine the butter, unsweetened chocolate, bittersweet chocolate, and espresso powder. Let the mixture melt over low heat, stirring occasionally. Remove and let cool slightly.

3. In a medium bowl, whisk the eggs and sugars together until smooth and pale. Add the olive oil, vanilla, and salt, and whisk until combined. Add the melted chocolate mixture and whisk until combined. Fold in the flour and the chopped semisweet chocolate and mix until just combined.

4. Scrape the batter into the prepared pan and smooth the top. Bake until the sides are slightly puffed and set but the center is still a bit gooey, about 25 minutes. Be brave: Underbaking the brownies is one of the secrets to their fudgy texture. Cool the brownies in the pan on a wire rack, about 2 hours, then refrigerate them for 30 minutes.

5. Make the glaze: In a medium heat-proof bowl set over a pan of simmering water, combine ¼ of the chocolate chips and the oil. Stir until the chocolate is melted and smooth. Add the remaining chips, remove from the heat, and stir until smooth. Let cool for 5 minutes. Pour the glaze over the brownies. Sprinkle with the bread crumbs. Let set for at least 10 minutes before serving.

Olive Oil–Toasted Bread Crumbs

MAKES ABOUT ¾ CUP

2 tablespoons mild extra-virgin olive oil

¾ cup fresh whole-wheat bread crumbs

1 teaspoon sugar

Pinch of fine sea salt

In a small sauté pan, heat the oil over medium heat until it begins to shimmer. Add the bread crumbs and toast, stirring constantly, until light golden brown, about 5 minutes. Stir in the sugar and salt and cook until slightly caramelized, 2 minutes. Transfer to a plate and let cool completely.

PER TABLESPOON: Calories **49**; Protein **1g**; Carbohydrates **5g**; Dietary Fiber **0g**; Sugar **1g**; Total Fat **3g**; Saturated Fat **0g**

Roasted Fruits with Coconut Whipped Cream and Amaretti Crisp

SERVES 6

1 (14-ounce) can full-fat coconut milk, refrigerated for 24 hours

2 tablespoons agave syrup or honey

1 teaspoon pure vanilla extract

2 pounds overly ripe stone fruits (plums, peaches, apricots), quartered and pitted

2 teaspoons cornstarch

Juice of 1 lemon

2 tablespoons sugar

1 vanilla bean, split lengthwise, seeds scraped

8 Amaretti cookies, coarsely crushed

PER SERVING: Calories **240**; Protein **4g**; Carbohydrates **33g**; Dietary Fiber **3g**; Sugar **26g**; Total Fat **11g**; Saturated Fat **10g**

By now you know that roasting is a foolproof way to get the sweetest, most intensely fruity flavor out of fruit, as it brings out their natural sugars and concentrates their flavors. Add luscious coconut whipped cream and Amaretti cookies, which are made with egg whites, for extra flavor and texture.

1. Ten minutes before you are ready to whip the coconut cream, put the mixing bowl and whisk attachment in the freezer to chill.

2. Remove the can of coconut milk from the refrigerator without shaking or tipping it. Remove the lid of the can and carefully, using a spoon, scoop the thick layer of coconut cream from the top and transfer it to the chilled mixing bowl. (Reserve the coconut water that has settled to the bottom of the can for another use.)

3. Whip the cream on medium speed until light and fluffy. Add the agave syrup and vanilla extract and continue to whip until incorporated. Cover and refrigerate until ready to use.

4. Preheat the oven to 375°F.

5. Put the fruit into a 9-inch baking dish and mix in the cornstarch, lemon juice, sugar, and vanilla bean and seeds. Set the baking dish on a rimmed baking sheet. Roast until the fruit is soft and the juices are bubbly and thickened, about 30 minutes.

6. Remove from the oven, scatter the cookies over the top, and return to the oven for 5 minutes.

7. Remove and let cool a little until warm, about 20 minutes. Serve the fruit in bowls, topping each serving with a dollop of the coconut cream.

Peaches in Sparkling Wine

SERVES 4

4 ripe peaches, halved, pitted, and thinly sliced

2 tablespoons honey

2 cups sparkling wine, such as Prosecco

Thinly sliced fresh basil or mint (optional)

PER SERVING: Calories **182**; Protein **1g**; Carbohydrates **30g**; Dietary Fiber **3g**; Sugar **22g**; Total Fat **0g**; Saturated Fat **0g**; Alcohol **7g**

As a whole, Italians aren't into overly sweet desserts; they are content to end a meal with a piece of perfectly ripe fruit and a bowl of nuts or this simple preparation of peaches macerated in sparkling wine. Nectarines and plums also work well here, as do berries, but don't try this with sub-par produce. The fruit must be truly ripe and flavorful to make a meaningful impression.

1. Put the peaches in a medium bowl, add the honey, and stir to combine. Let sit at room temperature for 15 minutes.

2. Add the wine, making sure to cover the peaches completely. Cover the bowl and refrigerate for at least 1 hour and up to 8 hours.

3. Serve the peaches and some of their marinade in goblets or bowls, topped with basil if desired.

Acknowledgments

Special thanks to:

Stephanie Banyas, it has been a pleasure working side by side with you for the past twenty years. Thank you for all of your hard work on every project that I throw your way . . . especially my cookbooks. I couldn't do it without you.

Sally Jackson, thank you for capturing my voice better than anyone, for your impeccable taste, and for never losing your cool.

Elyse Tirrell, for helping whenever and wherever needed on this book.

Ed Anderson, thank you for being so easy to work with and for your beautiful photos.

Pablo Muñoz
Renee Forsberg
Sean Rainaldi
Kerry Miller
Marysarah Quinn
Ian Dingman
Kate Tyler
Jana Branson
Stephanie Davis
Mark McCauslin

Kim Tyner
Andrea Portanova
Marjorie Livingston
Maeve Sheridan
Dahlia Warner
Courtney Fuglein
Bullfrog & Baum
Irika Slavin
Lauren Mueller
Laurence Kretchmer

Food Network
Rock Shrimp Productions
Vitamix
AllClad
KitchenAid
DeLonghi
Oxo

And, as always . . . last but not least: Rica Allannic, you are simply the best editor, better than all the rest. Thank you.

Index

Note: Page references in *italics* indicate photographs.